An Altitude SuperGuide

BC Ferries
and the
Canadian West Coast

An Altitude SuperGuide

BC Ferries

and the Canadian West Coast
the

by David Spalding,
Andrea Spalding,
and
Lawrence Pitt

•

Altitude Publishing Canada Ltd.
Canadian Rockies/Vancouver

Publication Information

Altitude Publishing Canada Ltd.
1500 Railway Avenue, PO Box 1410
Canmore, Alberta T0L 0M0

Extreme care has been taken to ensure that all information presented in this book is accurate and up to date, and neither the author nor the publisher can be held responsible for any errors.

Canadian Cataloguing in Publication Data
Spalding, David A.E., 1937–
BC Ferries and the Canadian West Coast

(SuperGuide)
Includes index.
ISBN 1-55153-605-X

1. British Columbia—Guidebooks.
2. Ferries—British Columbia—Guidebooks.
3. British Columbia Ferry Corporation.
I. Spalding, David A. E., 1937– II. Title. III. Series.
FC3807.P57 1995   917.1104'4   C94-910964-9
F1087.P57 1995

Made in Western Canada
Printed and bound in Canada
by Friesen Printers, Altona, Manitoba.

Altitude GreenTree Program
Altitude Publishing will plant in Canada twice as many trees as were used in the manufacturing of this product.

Front cover photos: Superferry

Frontispiece: Superferry approaching the dock

Back cover photo: Sunset over Mayne & Pender islands

Project Development

Concept/Art Direction	Stephen Hutchings
Design	Stephen Hutchings, Sandra Davis
Editing	Stephen Hutchings, Penny E. Grey
Maps	Catherine Burgess
Electronic Page Layout	Sandra Davis
Financial Management	Laurie Smith
Index/proofreading	Penny E. Grey

A Note from the Publisher
The world described in Altitude SuperGuides is a unique and fascinating place. It is a world filled with surprise and discovery, beauty and enjoyment, questions and answers. It is a world of people, cities, landscape, animals, and wilderness as seen through the eyes of those who live in, work with, and care for this world. The process of describing this world is also a means of defining ourselves.

It is also a world of relationship, where people derive their meaning from a deep and abiding contact with the land—as well as from each other. And it is this sense of relationship that guides all of us at Altitude to ensure that these places continue to survive and evolve in the decades ahead.

Altitude SuperGuides are books intended to be used, as much as read. Like the world they describe, *Altitude SuperGuides* are evolving, adapting, and growing. Please write to us with your comments and observations, and we will do our best to incorporate your ideas into future editions of these books.

Stephen Hutchings
Publisher

Contents

The **BC Ferries and the Canadian West Coast SuperGuide** is organized according to the following colour scheme:

Information and introductory sections . . . .

The Working Ferry . . . .

Getting to Vancouver Island . . . .

Island Hopping . . . .

Sunshine Coast . . . .

Cruising the Inside Passage . . . .

Queen Charlotte Islands . . . .

Reference and Index . . . .

1. Introduction

Spirit of British Columbia *arrives at Swartz Bay*

The BC Ferries, one of the largest ferry systems in the world, carries more than 22 million passengers a year—a figure approaching the population of Canada—on more than 40 vessels. For every passenger, a ferry ride can be the passport to a land of romance, showing many glimpses of spectacular scenery, fascinating history, and a vigorous and varied West Coast lifestyle.

True, some residents of the many islands served by the system treat a ferry ride as a routine fact of their existence, a daily trip to school or a weekly trip for groceries. Yet when the sun sparkles on the water, even the most jaded travellers pause and remember why they chose to live on an island in the first place.

Occasional users tend to treat the ferry as mass transit between cities—a more or less entertaining break in routine, a chance to read the paper or catch up on some sleep. Yet when the Captain draws attention to a pod of orcas, there is an eager rush to the side, as city dwellers seek contact with creatures that are free to roam the wild waters.

For any passenger, the world opened up by BC Ferries is full of excitement, offering the chance to meet people from around the world and experience some of B.C.'s striking landscape, the exciting natural world of the temperate rain forest, and waters with huge fish and far-travelled sea birds. The ferry system is the highway for the B.C. coast. It links Vancouver Island and the province's capital, Victoria, with the mainland of British Columbia by several routes. It provides the only public access to the islands of the Strait of Georgia and Howe Sound, and it crosses the inlets of the Sunshine Coast. From northern Vancouver Island (and occasionally Tsawwassen) it provides the only public transport through huge and spectacular areas of the Inside Passage to the communities of Bella Bella

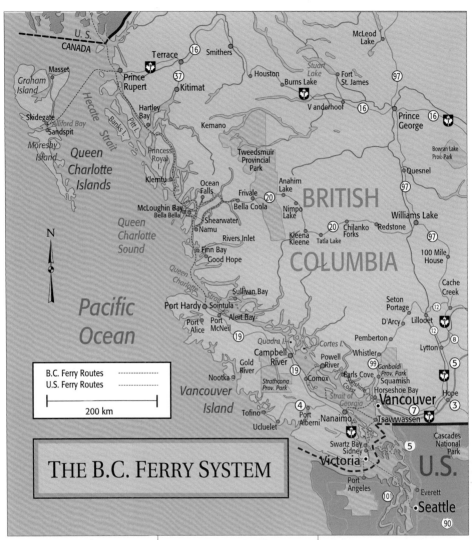

THE B.C. FERRY SYSTEM

and Prince Rupert. From there you can cross to the Queen Charlotte Islands (Haida Gwaii), the most isolated region of the province accessible by frequent boat service. The ferries will take you to places you can otherwise only reach by owning or chartering a boat or travelling by expensive cruise liner.

How to Use the SuperGuide

This book presents a brief overview of the ferry system and the area it covers, and tells you in greater detail how to access its services and make the best of a ferry trip, whether it be a 30-minute commuter ride or the adventure of a lifetime up the Inside Passage and across to the land of the Haida. We have tried to combine the basic "how to" information

you need to take a ferry trip with some hints of the magic that the area has—its history and nature, literature and visual art that have made this area so attractive for so long. Brief profiles of people are included, to give you an idea of the sort of people you may meet working or travelling on the ferry system, or living in the area.

Chapter 2 gives advice on using the ferry system. Chap-

Sunrise off starboard on the **Queen of Vancouver**

ters 3 to 5 provide background on the region as well as the system as a whole—things you may see from the ships, a historical overview of BC Ferries, and a brief account of the workings of the ships and the ferry system.

The remaining chapters present an overview of the major regions served by the ferries, moving from south to north. Thus we start in Chapters 6 to 8 with the major routes by which Vancouver Island is directly connected to the Lower Mainland, then give more detailed accounts of the islands of the Gulf and Queen Charlotte Sound. The route north along the Sunshine Coast from Vancouver and then across to Comox is separately covered.

On deck of the **Queen of Vancouver**

Chapters 9 and 10 cover the longer northern routes: the Inside Passage cruise from Port Hardy to Prince Rupert,

and the services to and on the Queen Charlotte Islands. A reference section brings together key addresses and phone numbers, and recommends additional reading about the region.

We have tried to be as accurate and up to date as possible, but travellers should be aware that BC Ferries is entering into a period of rapid change, as new terminals, ferries, and services are developed. The tourist industry, too, is rapidly developing, and individual attractions may have changed by the time of your visit. There is no substitute for talking to the BC Ferries and tourist offices in the areas you are planning to visit.

2. Planning Your Trip

How to Contact BC Ferries

Telephone:
Reservations and information (7 am to 10 pm daily)
- Victoria (604) 386-3431 fax (604) 381-5452
- Vancouver (604) 669-1211
- Salt Spring (604) 537-9921
- Southern Gulf Islands (604) 629-3215

Information:
24-hour recorded information for Mainland–Vancouver Island:
- Nanaimo (604) 753-6626
- Vancouver (604) 277-0277
- Victoria (604) 386-3431

Internet:
- http://bcferries.bc.ca/ferries

Address:
- British Columbia Ferry Corporation, 1112 Fort Street, Victoria, B.C., Canada V8V 4V2

Reservations

Reservations are required for:
- Tsawwassen–Southern Gulf Island
- Port Hardy–Prince Rupert
- Prince Rupert–Queen Charlotte Island routes
- Discovery Coast Passage

Tickets

- payment can be made by cash, cheque, or major credit card
- BC Senior Citizens (must present ID) can travel free (passenger only) on Monday through Thursday (except statutory holidays)
- discounts are available for some groups by advance arrangements

Schedules

Printed schedules are available for the following routes:
- Inside Passage–Queen Charlotte Islands
- Mainland–Vancouver Island–Sunshine Coast
- Northern Gulf Islands
- Southern Gulf Islands
- Discovery Coast Passage

Departures

October to May
- during off season, arrive at the terminal 30 to 40 minutes prior to departure

June to September
- some of the routes are heavily used in the summer months. Contact the BC Ferry Corporation regarding waiting times

Vehicle Classifications

- let the ticket agent know if your vehicle is more than 6'8" high or over 20' long

Food Service

- Superferries serve hot meals; some have buffets
- short run ferries are equipped with snack bars

Special Needs

- discounts are available for people with permanent disabilities, as well as their required companions. A special status ID card is needed.
- most ferries are equipped with wheelchair-accessible washrooms, and elevators or ramps

Children

- children under 12 must be accompanied by an adult
- baby change stations are available in both the men's and women's restrooms
- kids' play areas are available on some ferries

Pets

- pets must remain in your vehicle or on the car deck

Bus Routes

- Greyhound Lines Vancouver (604) 662-3222
- Maverick Coach Lines (604) 662-8051
- Pacific Coach Lines Vancouver (604) 662-8074, Victoria (604) 385-4411

Travel information

- Discover British Columbia 1-800-663-6000 provides general information and a reservation service, including provincial maps, travel and accommodation guides, and some regional information. It is generally useful to supplement this with information from local travel infocentres, included in the provincial publications.
- Port Hardy and District Chamber of Commerce (604) 949-7622, fax (604) 949-6653
- Queen Charlotte Travel Infocentre (604) 559-4742, fax (604) 559-8188

3. Fjords, Fog, Fish, and Freighters

Night voyages on the BC Ferries have their own magic

From the decks of the ferries you have a grandstand view of spectacular landscapes, a constantly changing wildlife, and human habitats that vary from one of the world's most spectacular cities to endless wilderness. Everywhere the ferries go, the sea is defined by land. Even in Hecate Strait, land is in sight. From barely emergent reefs to 13,000-foot mountains, the ferry routes present a constant procession of spectacular scenery. Many of the ferry routes run in the area geologists call the Coastal Trough, an area of low ground and shallow sea between two mountain ranges. In the west, the Insular Mountains run through Vancouver Island (the highest peak, Golden Hinde, at 7,219 feet), and the Queen Charlotte Islands (the highest at 3,700 feet). The mainland coast is marked by the Coast Mountains, running north from Vancouver and beyond the northern boundary of the province. A network of deep channels within the Coast Mountains have been flooded by seawater, creating the Inside Passage, one of the most spectacular fjords in the world. Here ships can sail among islands in a narrow passage sheltered from the often boisterous waters of the misnamed Pacific Ocean. The Olympic Mountains and the Cascades (with the conspicuous Mount Baker) continue south into the United States.

The apparent solidity of these rocks is misleading. In recent years, B.C.'s complex mountain chains and adjacent oceans have been analyzed in great detail, and have provided a testing ground for the development of new theories of sea-floor spreading, plate tectonics, and mountain building. The western mountains are part of the Wrangellia and Alexander terrares—chunks of rock that have a long history of drifting north and south be-

A view of one of the ferries from inside a tent

fore becoming part of North America some 60 million years ago. Poised on plate boundaries, these mountains are still unstable, a part of the Pacific "ring of fire." The spectacular eruption of Mount St. Helens just over the border in the U.S.A. reminds us that there are active volcanoes in the area, and occasional small earthquakes keep residents on their toes, waiting for the anticipated "big one" that may happen tomorrow—or be delayed for a couple of centuries.

During the last million years or so, massive glaciers built up on the Coast Ranges, and (with warmer intervals) remained until a mere 10,000 years ago. At its peak, the ice was approximately 8,000 feet thick over the site of Vancouver, flowing out of the Fraser Valley and across the Gulf Islands and southern Vancouver Island. It was split by the Olympic Mountains into two lobes, one flowing out through the Strait of Juan de Fuca to the Pacific, and the other bulldozing out Puget Sound. The whole area was depressed under this weight and is still slowly rising, producing raised beaches. V-shaped river valleys were gouged out by the glaciers to form the steep-sided U-shaped valleys, which now—flooded by the sea—provide passage for the ferries. High on the hillsides, lesser glaciers developed on the side slopes, deepening other valleys that have been truncated, their streams now cascading down in spectacular waterfalls.

Since the ice melted, wind, rain, rivers, and sea have been at work, nibbling at cliffs, tumbling rocks downhill, and forming beaches and bottom deposits. North of Tsawwassen, the great Fraser River brings huge amounts of sediment down from the interior mountains, building its delta seaward at the rate of 28 feet a year, and colouring the sea for a considerable distance from its mouth.

Fog, Rain, and Sunshine

BC Ferry country offers a variety of weather, and part of the pleasure of a voyage is to watch the ever changing cloudscape. Though the westernmost coast and highest country can be very wet, the lower areas of the Strait of Georgia and Inside Passage have the heaviest rainfall in a few months of the winter. Summer days can be glorious and hot, though sometimes early morning mist and fog can persist until noon. Later in the year, it can last longer. The

Crows in the Queue

WHILE QUEUING for the ferry, you are likely to have company—the elegant little northwestern crow has learned that ferry terminals provide easy pickings, and gathers in large numbers to scrounge whatever it can pick up. Though sometimes regarded as a small race of the American crow, sometimes as a separate species, this cheeky bird is not interested in what the experts think. More concerned with filling its belly, it will wander between vehicles and feet, land on the ferry deck and check the load in your truck, and—given half a chance—take off with your sandwich (before or after you have finished with it). During what is sometimes a long wait, the crows provide entertaining company, and may prompt interesting speculations about the evolution of new habits in birds—and people.

Orcas attract visitors from around the world

folklore of the coast tells of a fisherman who was stuck at sea in a fog on his wedding day. The fog was so thick, however, that he was able to walk across it to the church and get married. It was a full two years later, after the birth of his first child, that the weather cleared up and he found out that not only had he reached the wrong village, but he had married the wrong girl!

Snow lies mainly on the high mountain ranges, forming a spectacular backdrop to the landscape even in summer. Occasional heavy snowfalls occur on lower ground, but the warmest areas (such as southern Vancouver Island and the Gulf Islands) have few snow falls—though they can disrupt transport in a way that rarely happens in Canada's colder climates.

On the water, there is often a cool breeze, even in sheltered waters, so it is wise to have a sweater on hand, even on warm days. Where passages are open to the Pacific, there is always the chance of a storm, and even inland waters can be lively if the wind gets up. Seasickness remedies are rarely necessary unless you are particularly susceptible.

Shipping adds its own life to the water, and waves from the ferry wake can make life exciting for small craft. Logs float everywhere, and are a hazard to smaller vessels. Some have fallen in from eroding coasts or river banks, others have escaped from log booms. Worst are the "deadheads"—waterlogged logs that float vertically and are almost invisible in rough seas.

Fish, Eagles, and Orcas

The sea is full of life; indeed this area sustains a rich fishery, an abundant bird fauna, and one of the most studied (and watched) whale populations in the world. Every moment you are on deck there is likely to be something to see.

When the water is clear and the light is right, you may be able to see jellyfish drifting below the surface, and, close to shore, the ropes of giant kelp. Spectacular purple and orange seastars form colourful constellations on the rocks. Schools of fish dart in the depths, and large salmon often jump out of the water. When the salmon are biting, boats of sports fishermen cluster at

Mountains and clouds

favoured spots, such as the ends of Active Pass. Seals are abundant, and may be seen popping their round heads up by the ferry terminals, or hauled out on rocks in apparently uncomfortable positions. The even larger Steller's sea lions gather at favoured places, such as Nanaimo Harbour.

In the sheltered waters, pods of orcas may be seen flashing their white sides as they roll out of the water to breathe. The 300 orcas of the Strait of Georgia region are among the best studied whales in the world; individual pods and their members have been identified and named by repeated photographs of their varied dorsal fins. As well as scientists, they attract large numbers of whale watchers, who sail from various ports to observe their antics. Most of the orca pods occupy a fairly stable territory, and live largely on fish. A few groups seem to be perpetual transients, and live up to their older name of "killer whale" by attacking seals and larger whales. Other whale species occur in the area, including Pacific white-sided dolphin and Dall's porpoise. Occasionally larger whales such as the humpback or gray whale stray into the Inside Passage; the Captain is likely to point them out to lucky passengers.

Among the most conspicuous birds are groups of cormorants hitching a ride on a passing log, often with their wings hung out to dry. Schools of herring may attract a feeding frenzy of gulls. The most common is the glaucous-winged gull, but about another dozen large species may be seen by the careful watcher. The huge bald eagles often

Last Keeper of the Light?

JEAN BEAUDOT is one of the 60 or so individuals who tend the 35 light stations on the coast of British Columbia. A lightkeeper since 1975, Jean and his wife were attracted to the west coast from their native Quebec by the beauty and isolation that a light station offers and the opportunity to raise their young family in a very close-knit environment. Jean began his love affair with the ocean and lighthouses at the remote station at Green Island, on the north coast near the Alaska boundary.

Several years spent at the windswept Langara Light Station in storm-battered Dixon Entrance was a highlight in Jean's 20-year career. There, both children were schooled by their parents, with help from a correspondence school. Education involved the usual language, math, and science, but it was augmented with learning to dive and, each year, extended two-month explorations along the coast aboard the family's 30-foot boat. Although French was the working language in the home, television reception from Prince Rupert, even on a remote light station, "taught" the children English at an early age.

Now at the Active Pass Light Station on Mayne Island, this is the first time the family has lived "in civilization." Jean's daily routine at the light station involves rounds of the buildings and grounds to ensure everything is in good working order.

Daily visiting hours for the public bring an estimated 10,000 visitors each year to this station on Georgina Point, and Jean is there to answer questions and to provide boating safety information to the many people who come. The attraction that a lighthouse has for people is deeply rooted. Jean feels that a lighthouse "gives one a good feeling-one of safety." Light keepers like Jean maintain a vigilant watch for local mariners. The marine VHF radio is on 24 hours a day in the home so that Jean or another family member can be alerted to a distress situation immediately.

Alas, Jean and his fellow keepers may be the last act of a long-standing drama. The Coast Guard has announced that all light stations on the coast will be automated very soon and the diligent human keepers replaced. The light will still be on, but no one will be at home to answer a call for help.

join the whirling birds; not only will they catch fish, but they eat large numbers of gulls. Flocks of little Bonaparte's gulls build up in Active Pass and other sheltered waters in late summer. Large flocks of murres, murrelets, and auks raft in the water, and loons and grebes are abundant in fall and winter, though they can be hard to identify in non-breeding plumage. Several species of ducks gather in open water or sheltered bays, and flocks of snow and brant geese can be seen in season.

Many seabirds nest on islands and cliffs, decorating the rocks below the nests with extensive whitewash. Ospreys and bald eagles build large nests high in trees, and these can often be seen from the ferry. When they are resting, the white heads of adult birds often stand out conspicuously against the dark green trees. Rocky islands attract the striking black oystercatcher, and muddy flats are often punctuated with motionless herons.

Away from the settled areas, all but the steepest slopes are generally covered with dense forest; very little has been cut along the Inside Passage. Bare trees show the results of old crown fires, which have rejuvenated the forest into what seems from a distance to be a rich surface of green velvet. Few coniferous trees can be recognized indi-vidually, though they include species as different as hemlocks, Douglas firs, cedars, spruces and firs. Patches of the deciduous red alders can be striking, particularly in spring

Historic lighthouse, Kuper Island

and fall. Along the shores of southern Vancouver Island and the Gulf Islands, the sturdy Garry oak and tortuous red-stemmed arbutus can often be picked out from the deck. Smaller plants are harder to identify even with binoculars, but masses of the introduced yellow-flowered broom may catch the eye.

Even from the ferry deck you can get occasional glimpses of land birds and mammals. The small black-tailed deer sometimes comes to the shore, otters often swim along the beaches, and mink and raccoons are fearless foragers among the rocks and tidelines.

Buoys and Lighthouses

When you are at sea, the most important features of the landscape to the crew, and perhaps most interesting to the traveller, are the navigation aids that make a safe passage possible. Everywhere along the route are buoys marking safe passages or warning of submerged hazards. At night the network of lighthouses—each with its unique pattern of flashes—is most apparent.

Although they seem an essential part of the landscape, the development of the lighthouse network has been slow and hazardous. Authorities in Ottawa have not been quick to pay for the construction of a new light; often the trigger has been a major wreck.

Early light stations were put up in the late nineteenth century. For example, Georgina Point on Mayne Island was erected in 1895, and had its first keeper, Henry Georgeson, for 37 years; his children and grandchildren continued in the service of other light stations for nearly 60 years. Gradually the light-station network was extended,

Freighter in Plumper Sound

and a body of dedicated, sometimes eccentric, and always hard working men and women became associated with the service. They had to put up with isolation, poor equipment, rigid regulations, and frequently dangerous seas. Their story is a fascinating one. As well as their basic duties of operating lights and fog warning systems, the keepers have rescued many sailors in danger of shipwreck, and made important weather and natural science observations. After more than a century, plans are being made to replace the lighthouse keepers with mechanical equipment.

Freighters, Self Dumpers, and Catamarans

BC Ferries share the waters with a great variety of other craft—a shipwatcher's delight. Some of the ferries travel along or across major shipping lanes, others through narrow channels little used by other traffic. Close to the major ports of Vancouver, Victoria, and Prince Rupert, in some of the busiest inland waters in the

world, there is almost always something to see. Vessels going your way can be studied at leisure; those going in the opposite direction may only be in sight for a short time.

You can often see other ferries, particularly at large terminals, where several routes converge. There are several overlapping routes in the southern islands; often two or three other ferries are in sight at the same time. Other passenger vessels include the tiny water taxis that ferry kids to school and the elegant cruise ships that ply the Inside Passage to Alaska. Specialized passenger vessels are used for whale watching.

Some freighters, tankers, and container ships that travel the world load at Roberts Bank by Tsawwassen, and others often tie up outside the port of Vancouver and in Plumper Sound. Smaller containers and cargoes of sawdust or wood chips are carried by barges, whereas rafts, towed slowly along by tug boats, move cranes and pile-drivers.

An occasional commercial fishing boat can be seen at

most times, but when an "opening" of a specific fishery is expected, they may be travelling in a pack, or actively fishing along the ferry route. Watch for seiners, gillnetters and trollers, specialized for different catches of salmon, halibut or herring respectively, and working in different ways, with lines trailing from nets hauled over the stern of the vessel.

Other kinds of working vessel are represented by the grey ships of the Canadian Navy, often seen on training voyages or exercises, and the orange vessels used by the Coast Guard service patrols.

Watch for recreational vessels of all kinds—fancy power cruisers, sporty speedsters and outboard-powered rowboats or zodiacs, windsurfers out in the middle of the Strait of Georgia, and yachts, catamarans and trimarans. Some of the sailboats never go more than a few miles from the home marina, but others—no larger or more impressive—have battered their way around the world. When there is a good breeze and the ferry passes a round-the-island race, a dozen or more vivid spinnakers make a terrific sight.

Also be on the watch for heritage vessels: old fashioned steam yachts and converted fishing vessels that are still afloat; lovingly cared for after decades of useful life in some other calling. On occasion, you may catch sight of a tall ship: an old or recently constructed sailing vessel that preserves the traditional style of sailing.

Although the ship is still the primary means of travel, hovercraft, helicopters, and float planes are also important. It is not uncommon to be able to watch tiny planes landing

Bald eagle

and taking off at the same time as the ferries are docking, Helicopters and Coast Guard hovercraft are important in rescue operations.

Ports, Pulp Mills, and Packing Plants

The traditional industries of agriculture, fishing, mining, and lumber are still important in British Columbia, though the resources are often fewer. Century-old orchards on the Gulf Islands, and the market gardens and fields around Tsawwassen, remind us of some of the past and present food sources of adjacent cities. Old fish plants are visible close to the shore, and restored ones may be seen as museums at Steveston in the Fraser estuary, and near

Prince Rupert on the Skeena River. Mining is mainly located at inland sites, but old mines may be seen at Britannia Beach in Howe Sound. Channels off the Inside Passage serve the aluminum plant at Kitimat. Patches of cleared timber—the notorious clearcuts—are visible on many hillsides, though as these regenerate from natural or planted reforestation they gradually blend with the remaining forest again. Old style lumbermen often worked from floating bases on this coast: bunk- and cookhouses built on rafts, which could be towed to a new base as the timber was worked out.

The many freighters are evidence of the importance of B.C. as an ocean gateway to Asia and other destinations across the Pacific. Evidence of major transportation activity can be seen in the coal-loading facilities at Roberts Bank, and the huge grain elevators at Prince Rupert.

Southern areas adjacent to the ferry routes are heavily residential. The city of Vancouver, the Lower Mainland, the southern part of Vancouver Island, as well as the Gulf Islands, are growing faster than any other area of Canada. Along with the resident population, the development of tourism adds many people to the summer scene; you will find many fellow passengers on the ferries from Japan and Europe, as well as North America, and not a few from more distant parts.

4. Highlights of History

Expert users of the water highway

Many and varied vessels have plied the coastal waters of British Columbia during the past few thousand years. For the vast majority of this time, native peoples navigated the 17,000 mi of shoreline, reefs, and passages in canoes. Explorers from Spain and England preceded settlement. Settlement brought the ships of the Hudson's Bay and the British Navy. Later ships served growing communities along the coast and linked Canada with Asia. The water highway we travel today in modern ferries is linked to this rich history.

5500–1500 years ago - Salish-type culture present on the Gulf Islands, presumably using canoes.

1592 - a Greek, known as Juan de Fuca, aboard a Spanish vessel, is reputed to have explored the entrance to the great strait that now bears his name.

18th Century

1778 - Captain Cook lands at Nootka Sound.

1792 - Captain Vancouver meets the Spanish explorers Galiano and Valdes near Vancouver.

19th Century

1837 - Hudson's Bay Company *Beaver*, the first steam-powered vessel on the coast, explores southern Vancouver Island waters.

1843 - Fort Victoria established.

1846 - Oregon Treaty signed; the Hudson's Bay Company begins to move to Vancouver Island.

1849 - Crown Colony of Vancouver Island established by Sir James Douglas and control granted to the Hudson's Bay Company.

1850 - Gold discovered in Queen Charlotte Islands.

1852 - James Douglas appointed Lieutenant Governor of the Queen Charlotte Islands; American Vessel, the *Susan Sturges*, plundered by Haidas.

1857 - USS *Active* together with HMS *Plumper* (Captain Richards) survey the international boundary. Many local place names come from this survey, including Active Pass.

1858 - Fraser gold rush leads miners to row from Victoria through the Gulf Islands. Miner's Bay was a stop on this journey.

1859 - Americans shoot a Hudson's Bay pig on San Juan Island, the only casualty in a simmering boundary dispute named the Pig War.

1862 - William Duncan founds Metlakatla, a model Christian Tsimshian village near what is now Prince Rupert. It became famous because it was untouched by the smallpox epidemic that devastated many other native settlements.

1865 - Britain fails to purchase Alaska panhandle.

1866 - Colony of British Columbia established.

1867 - Confederation of Canada; Americans buy Alaska.

1871 - British Columbia enters Confederation on the promise of a railroad link.

1872 - Loss of the bark *Zephyr* on Georgina Shoals, off Georgina Point, Mayne Island.

1886 - First passenger train arrives on the west coast from Montreal.

1889 - B.C. Premier Amor De Cosmos proposes a ferry link between the tip of the Saanich Peninsula and the mainland, using vessels capable of a one hour and ten minute crossing.

1890 - S.S. *Cutch,* first Union Steamship Company vessel, arrives on the coast.

1891 - *Empress of India,* first of the great Canadian Pacific Railway white ships, arrives at Burrard Inlet.

1897 - Steamer *Portland* comes south with a ton of gold and started the Klondike Gold Rush. Thousands of people head for Yukon.

20th Century

1906 - Prince Rupert established.

1914 - Provincial government of Richard McBride purchases, for $1.5 million, two submarines to augment the inadequately equipped west coast navy during World War I. This was the first foray of the provincial government into ship owning.

1918 - Canadian Pacific operates the first car ferry on the coast—the *Island Princess.*

1923 - Canadian Pacific builds a second car ferry—the *Motor Princess*—at Esquimalt.

1925 - *Princess Marguerite* arrives with the capability of carrying 30 cars.

1930 - Gulf Island Ferry Corporation formed by an irate Victoria newspaper publisher upset with poor service to the

Bennett's Navy

IN THE LATE 1950s,' British Columbia's Premier, William Bennett, judged the ferry service between the mainland and Vancouver Island to be inadequate for a growing province with a bright future. Canadian Pacific Steamships grudgingly provided poor car ferry service and many long-time British Columbia residents remember midnight sailings and six-hour crossings between Victoria and Vancouver. The American Black Ball Line, although providing much better service than Canadian Pacific, mainly up the Sunshine Coast and from Horseshoe Bay to Nanaimo, did not seem willing to invest in the same future that the Premier saw—a future of economic expansion and population growth.

A serious labour dispute be-

Premier W.A.C. Bennett, creator of the BC Ferry Corporation.

tween the marine unions and Canadian Pacific Steamships threatened to isolate Vancouver

Island in the summer of 1958. When the Black Ball employees threatened to strike in sympathy, Premier Bennett acted swiftly. Empowered by the *Civil Defense Act,* and federal legislation, Bennett forced the disgruntled workers back into service. Then, when he determined that neither Canadian Pacific nor Black Ball had any plans for improving and expanding their ferry service, Bennett acted boldly, and announced that the government would take over the ferry service. His government built an entirely new ferry-system infrastructure, including new roll-on roll-off ferries and new terminals to go with them. From this bold beginning, the BC Ferries—long nicknamed "Bennett's Navy"—has grown to its present size.

A modern superferry plies the coastal waters

Gulf Islands; acquires *Island Princess* from Canadian Pacific Steamships and renames it the *Cy Peck*, after a decorated war hero.

1946 - "Sparky" New, a coastal shipping legend himself, creates Coast Ferries with the vessel *Brentwood*, running across Saanich Inlet to Mill Bay.

1951 - Gulf Islands Ferry Corporation taken over by Salt Spring Island businessman, Gavin Mouat; Captain Alexander Peabody, from Washington State, establishes the Black Ball Line, building terminals at Horseshoe Bay, Departure Bay, on the Sunshine Coast, and at Jervis Inlet. The vessels *Kahloke, Bainbridge, Quillayute, Chinook,* and *Smokwa* establish the Black Ball Line as a dependable service

1955 - Gulf Islands Ferry Corporation purchases *Motor Princess* from Canadian Pacific Steamships after obtaining a subsidy from the new Social Credit government of W.A.C. Bennett.

1956 - Coast Ferries builds the *Mill Bay* and another vessel named *Island Princess.*

1960 - MV *Sidney's* inaugural sailing on new ferry route between Tsawwassen and Swartz Bay.

1961 - BC Ferries purchases Gulf Islands Ferries and Black Ball assets.

1962 - Six *Queen of Victoria* class ferries built.

1966 - *Cy Peck* retires from a long service on the coast; *Queen of Prince Rupert* begins northern service.

1967 - *Queen of Prince Rupert* goes aground on Haddington Reef near Port McNeil.

1969 - Coast Ferries *Mill Bay* and *Island Princess* acquired by BC Ferries. *Island Princess* enlarged and renamed *North Island Princess.*

1970 - The *Queen of Victoria* collides with the Soviet Freighter *Sergey Yesenin* in Active Pass. Three passengers are killed.

1976 - Three *Queen of Cowichan*-class ferries are built; *Queen of Alberni* goes aground in Active Pass in Au-

gust.

1980 - *Queen of the North* joins the "Inside Passage" route and becomes the flag ship.

1981 - Two jumbo ferries, the *Queen of Oak Bay* and the *Queen of Surrey*, are built.

1987 - Canadian Pacific withdraws completely from coastal passenger shipping with the disposal of the *Princess of Vancouver.*

1990 - BC Ferries adds a fourth route across the Strait of Georgia from Tsawwassen to Departure Bay, near Nanaimo.

1992 - A loading accident on the *Queen of New Westminster* at Nanaimo in March results in the loss of three lives.

1993 - *Spirit of British Columbia*, first of the 2,000-passenger superferries is built and Tsawwassen and Swartz Bay terminals undergo major expansion and upgrading.

1994 - *Spirit of Vancouver Island*, a second superferry, is built and BC Ferries carries a record 22 million passengers and 8 million vehicles for the year.

5. The Working Ferry

The control tower operators view, Swartz Bay

Behind the scenes, BC Ferries is a complex organization that deserves to be better known. Each ship is a little world of its own, crewed by expert people, that must be able to function independently while at sea. As you enjoy your ferry ride, give a thought to the daunting task facing the ferry crew. Your ship must follow a tight schedule, sometimes connecting with other ferries, yet you are travelling through narrow waterways shared with an unpredictable number of other vessels and subject to the vagaries of weather and water. Your ship must move safely among natural obstacles and other water traffic to deliver its freight of vehicles and passengers. Considering the many things that could go wrong, BC Ferries operates with amazing success, and the system has a worldwide reputation for safety.

Each ship must provide passengers with information, food, refreshment, recreation, and a comfortable and safe passage. As a public carrier, BC Ferries has to meet many safety standards enforced by the Canadian Coast Guard. Among the 22 million passengers served each year, some need special help, cheerfully and professionally given by specially trained crews. BC Ferries is one of the largest ferry operators in the world, with over 40 vessels, 43 terminals, and 2,600 employees. This organization has to manage large amounts of money, order supplies—$22 million for diesel fuel alone—select, train and supervise staff, and acquire, manage, repair and service real estate and complex machines.

Where Do Ferries Come From?

Most of BC Ferries' fleet of 19 large and 23 small vessels were built in British Columbia. Victoria and Vancouver shipyards have been the birthplace of the majority of the fleet, although a few vessels have been purchased from other ferry fleets. The *Queen of the North*, for example, built in Germany, came from Sweden. All vessels, however, wear the distinctive colours of the Dogwood Fleet and are outfitted to meet the needs of this coast.

Building ferries is a complicated and capital-intensive task, requiring much time to plan and complete each vessel.

The luxury of time and money was not always available, so the BC Ferries developed innovative engineering solutions to increase the system capacity and meet the growing demand. In 1970, after only 10 years in business, all seven major vessels were stretched—each ferry was cut in half and a new midship section inserted—increasing vehicle and passenger carrying capacity. A similar but bolder feat of engineering was accomplished, beginning in 1981, when five of the stretched ferries were sliced lengthwise and raised by insertion of an entire vehicle deck. The *Queen of Esquimalt* originally had a vehicle capacity of 106 cars. After stretching and raising, the vessel now carries up to 376 cars and 1,360 passengers. This was cheaper and faster than building three additional ferries to achieve the same capacity.

Building new ferries continues to play a major part in meeting the demand for ferry travel. Much of the engineering skill and fleet knowledge cultivated from 30 years of experience went into the design and construction of the "S" Class superferries, the *Spirit of British Columbia* and the *Spirit of Vancouver Island*. These vessels can each carry 470 cars and 2,100 passengers. The increased passenger capacity reflects the growing trend of bus and foot passenger traffic experienced by the BC Ferries.

Before You Board

Arriving at a terminal you first encounter a **ticket agent**, who will determine your fare and issue tickets and boarding passes. If you are in a vehicle, you will be assigned a boarding lane with other vehicles, to

Finding the Way

HAVE YOU HAVE ever been aboard a ferry at night, looked up from your newspaper, and wondered why a crew member was putting up blinds on the windows of the forward lounge? The reason is that this helps to maintain the bridge crew's night vision—a crucial element in watch keeping. While you relax in a lounge or enjoy a meal, the Captain and officers on the bridge are keeping a diligent watch at all times. The key to a safe passage is, and always has been, a constant visual lookout. Modern sensors such as radar, satellite navigation, and depth sounders provide additional information for making decisions, and in conditions of poor visibility, the Captain must rely more heavily on the instrumentation. The most difficult condition to be in, according to one superferry Captain is night-time in fog. Finding a ferry dock at night in heavy fog, and completing the docking while compensating for the effects of wind and tidal currents, takes

Modern sensors provide accurate information

tremendous skill.

Good communication is also important for a ferry to find its way. All BC Ferries ships' crews maintain a "communication watch" on Channel 16, the calling and emergency channel used by most vessels worldwide. Over this channel, a ferry can ask about the intentions of another vessel, to help decide if a change of course is necessary. Many mariners call for help over this channel by issuing a mayday distress call. Each ferry maintains contact with its respective terminal, with weather broadcasts, and with another unseen hand—the Vessel Traffic System. Headquartered in Vancouver Harbour, this requires major vessels to check in and report their movements. A ferry checks in to the system by radio just before departure and can be updated about other vessels that will be traversing the ferry's intended course.

Making headway across the strait

await loading. If you are at one of the four major terminals (Tsawwassen, Horseshoe Bay, Departure Bay or Swartz Bay), each time another passenger or vehicle checks in, the information is instantly transmitted to the terminal control tower where, under the watchful eyes of the terminal **Control Tower Operators**, the passenger and vehicle limits for each ferry are carefully monitored. The control tower communicates with the terminal crew to maintain an orderly assembly of vehicles, and with the travelling public through announcements. The overall responsibility of the terminal operation resides with the **Terminal Manager**. The control tower will announce when the ferry is ready for loading, and the terminal crew will shortly direct the vehicles to the appropriate dock.

Operations at Sea

The romantic image of the Captain on the bridge is deeply rooted in the past thousand years of seafaring. To do the job today, however, a ferry Captain, charged with the responsibility of safe passage for the vessel, crew, and passengers, has already acquired many years of experience, and is backed up by other skilled and dedicated individuals, many of whom we, the travelling public, never see.

The ship's **Deck Department crew** direct the loading of the ferry. The **Chief Officer**, who heads the deck department, is responsible to the Captain for the safe and orderly loading (and unloading) of the ferry. When the vessel is fully loaded, the Chief Officer will request clearance from the control tower. Once this is received, the ramp will be raised and the Chief Officer will report to the Captain that the deck department is ready for sailing.

The **Catering Department**, supervised by the **Chief Steward** is probably the most public face of the crew. Besides providing food services from the cafeterias and snack bars, running retail services from the gift shops, and keeping the interior passenger areas clean and tidy, these vital crew members answer a multitude of questions from passengers and are a prime resource for a safe and comfortable trip. In addition to their normal duties, each member of the Catering Department is qualified to act in an emergency to augment the deck department, whether at life boat stations, crowd control, or medical emergencies. This is why the Chief Steward must report to the Captain, prior to each sailing, that the Catering Department is ade-

The One that Got Away

ON AUGUST 25, 1966 the *Queen of Burnaby* was preparing for the first sailing of the day from Departure Bay in Nanaimo. The engineers were warming up the engines long before the 8:00 am departure. The variable-pitch propellers were, for some unknown reason, not in the neutral position but instead were beginning to provide forward thrust to the ferry, which at Departure Bay was docked stern-to. The mooring lines eventually parted and the ferry sailed into the bay with no-one on the bridge. Fortunately the engineers discovered the mistake, stopped the engines and dropped anchor. A very surprised Captain was summoned from his home and taken by small boat to his wayward ferry, which he then docked in time for the scheduled departure.

John Van Tol, Chief Engineer

The engine room workshop

"YOU HAVE TO work your way up on one ship and stay with it over the long term. That way you get to know the sounds, smell, and vibration of the engine, and can hear or smell anything strange that's the start of a problem."

To make his point, John Van Tol proudly showed us a cracked engine part that he and his staff had replaced the day before. They caught it before the fatigued metal had completely broken off and caused thousands of dollars worth of damage.

John inhabits a rabbit warren of passages that burrow through a complex of pipes, engines, coils, compressors, and refrigeration and sewage plants down in the hull of the *Queen of the North*. The noise level and heat are overpowering, and ear muffs are needed for survival. It's a whole other world down there. The engineers have a workroom and two of everything, so when things go wrong they can be replaced. There's even an anvil and blacksmith shop so the engineers can make something on the spot.

"Passengers only ever hear of the major breakdowns, never of the incredible variety and successful "on the spot" repairs the crew troubleshoot before they become a major problem," laughed John ruefully. "A fault might slow the vessel down but it's rare for the ferry to have to stop. There's even a replica of the bridge controls down in the engine room. If anything goes wrong with the electronics so bridge control is lost, the vessel can be controlled from the engine room with visual commands from the bridge."

While we were touring the engine area, crew members were busy doing their hourly assessment of all valves, joins, and gauges, and marking the results down on clipboard forms that can be checked.

"Safety is a big factor in Canada, and B.C. in particular has one of the highest standards in the world for equipment safety," said John proudly. "In fact the Coast Guard inspections and regular upgrading of standards keep our accident level down to one of the best records in the world."

Passengers Without Tickets

BABIES BORN ON a BC Ferries vessel get a lifetime pass to the ferry route on which they made their unanticipated entrance. While the crew don't encourage such events, they certainly go out of their way to make the inevitable as safe as possible.

At one impending birth, the attending crew alerted electrical Officer Ray Jupe that they were going to need something to clamp the umbilical cord. Ray went through the workshops and couldn't find anything small or neat enough. He found a rather large clamp (one of the Chief Engineer's favourites) and carefully ground it down to a minute size, then cleaned off all the oil, and polished and ground it again so it had shiny surfaces. Then he sterilized it and took it up to the medical room. As it happens, it wasn't needed. Ray was then stuck with explaining to the Chief Engineer how his favorite large clamp had drastically shrunk in size.

Another staff member was even more directly involved. Ian McRae was mate on the tiny *Kwuna*, taking its 20-minute run across Skidegate Inlet. "We were in an overload situation and behind schedule, when in the midst of my duties, a hand clamped on my shoulder with a grip signifying sheer terror. A man proclaimed, 'My wife is having a baby in the washroom right now.' The next few minutes were the most panicked, scariest, excruciatingly long, and joyous minutes I've ever experienced."

quately staffed for the trip's passenger load.

Hidden from most of us, members of the **Engineering Department** keep many of the sophisticated ship's systems in proper working order. Under the direction of the **Chief Engineer**, the engineers maintain the various systems: engines that provide movement, generators that provide power and lighting, on-board sewage treatment systems, hot and cold water, heating and ventilation. The Chief Engineer can control these various services from the control room, while the engineering staff constantly maintain rounds of the machinery spaces, inspecting and providing routine maintenance. Occasionally the Engineering Department is called upon to deliver a minor engineering miracle to solve a mechanical problem before it in-

terferes with the ship's schedule. For these reasons, the Captain waits for a report from the Chief Engineer that the engineering systems are ready for sailing, before he or she begins the final checks of the vessel's status as seen from the sensors on the bridge. Only after all this checking will the Captain begin the sequence of events that allows the ferry to leave the dock and begin its journey.

After a ferry's last run of the night is completed, the crew is relieved by a skeleton crew of engineers who work through the night. The engineers perform regular maintenance that can only be done when most systems are shut down. Tanker trucks arrive and the ships fuel tanks are quietly replenished: a superferry consumes about 32,000 litres of diesel fuel per day.

Meanwhile, Back at the Office

Although to passengers, perhaps, the ferries and terminals are the BC Ferries, there is ac-

tually an important office component, in the Head Office in Victoria. Here the Reservation Service Information Centre provides information and takes your bookings. Fleet and Terminal Engineering and Operations managers are based there, along with the personnel, financial, environmental and other management staff that are essential to any large corporation with assets over $600 million and a budget around $300 million.

Major changes started in the early 1990s, with the two superferries, major expansions to Tsawwassen and Swartz Bay terminals, and new computer systems. A new 10 year capital plan was approved in 1994. Included are three "fast ferries," which can carry vehicles, as well as passengers, at 37 knots and a new northern ferry . A new terminal will be built in 1997 at Duke Point near Nanaimo, and there will be further enhancement of other main terminals.

How Many Muffins?

In 1994, the Ferries served:

Bacon (slices)	1,783,000
Bread (slices)	4,025,000
Chicken strips (portions)	534,179
Chocolate milk (glasses)	413,000
Coffee (regular cups)	10,392,000
Creamers	8,979,000
Doughnuts	355,860
Eggs	2,674,000
French fries (kg)	340,000
Hamburger patties	925,400
Milk (glasses)	1,247,000
Muffins	3,385,620
Pop (glasses)	2,097,000
Tea bags (regular)	3,685,000
Soup	1,054,980
Watermelon (kg)	23,587
Wieners	657,200
Yogurt (portions)	220,692

Give a Hoot—the Ship's Whistles

WHILE ABOARD THE ferry, you are likely to hear a ship's whistle or signal. What's the message?

- **One Long Blast**—If the ferry is docked at the terminal, one long blast means the ferry is about to depart. If the ferry is under way, one long blast is used as an alert to other vessels before the ferry rounds a bend, as it does in traversing Active Pass.
- **One Short Blast**—The ferry intends to turn to starboard (right). This is also the acknowledgment signal to other vessels.

- **Two Short Blasts**—The ferry intends to turn to port (left).
- **Three Short Blasts**—The ferry is reversing power, either to stop or to go astern.
- **Four or More Short Blasts**—The ferry is warning other vessels of danger or potential collision. This often happens when a ferry, for example, is entering Active Pass near Helen Point on Mayne Island (a popular fishing spot) or entering Horseshoe Bay or Nanaimo, both of which are often crowded with pleasure craft.

Whale watching is one of the delights while sailing on the BC Ferries

Sailing through Active Pass at night

6. Getting to Vancouver Island

Spirit of Vancouver Island, *the newest "S Class" ferry*

With Victoria, the capital city of British Columbia, and over half a million residents on Vancouver Island, and Vancouver, the province's biggest city and the rest of B.C.'s residents on the mainland, it is no wonder that the ferry crossings between the mainline and Vancouver Island are the major service provided by BC ferries, carrying about half the total traffic in the system.

Several alternative routes are in use. From Tsawwassen, south of Vancouver, a frequent ferry to Swartz Bay passes through the beautiful Southern Gulf Islands and provides access to Victoria and southern Vancouver Island. Also from Tsawwassen, the longer Mid-Island Express heads up the Strait of Georgia to the city of Nanaimo, which is also connected more directly to Horseshoe Bay, close to the entrance of Howe Sound, northwest of Vancouver. Further north, a shorter crossing connects Comox to Powell River. Lastly, the Port Hardy to Prince Rupert ferry through the Inside Passage also connects the mainland to Vancouver Island.

Tsawwassen to Swartz Bay

Tsawwassen terminal sees the highest number of visitors, as it serves no less than seven destinations. In a daring move, the terminal was built out into the sea in 1960. It has been extended in recent years, and now has capacity for 2,500 vehicles waiting at any given time for Swartz Bay, Nanaimo, and Gulf Islands ferries. Repairs are done not far away at Deas Island in the Fraser River. In summer, an artists' marketplace provides a variety of arts and crafts for demonstration and sale. While you are waiting you can enjoy the views, and perhaps put in a little bird watching.

To the north of the terminal, on a similar artificial

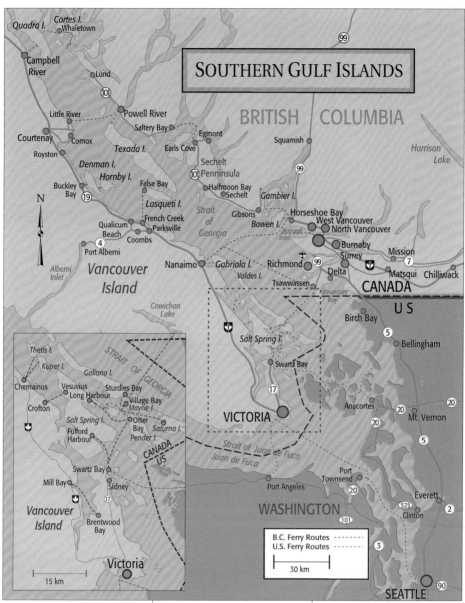

SOUTHERN GULF ISLANDS

BRITISH COLUMBIA

Quadra I. Cortes I. Whaletown

Campbell River

Lund

Little River

Powell River

Saltery Bay

Egmont

Courtenay

Comox

Texada I.

Earls Cove

Squamish

Harrison Lake

Royston

Denman I.

Hornby I.

False Bay

Sechelt

Penninsula

Buckley Bay

Halfmoon Bay

Sechelt

Gambier I.

Lasqueti I.

Qualicum Beach

French Creek

Parksville

Coombs

Gibsons

Bowen I.

Horseshoe Bay

West Vancouver

North Vancouver

Burrard Inlet

Burnaby

Mission

Port Alberni

Alberni Inlet

Vancouver Island

Strait of Georgia

Nanaimo

Gabriola I.

Valdes I.

Richmond

Surrey

Matsqui Chilliwack

Delta

Tsawwassen

CANADA

Cowichan Lake

Boundary Bay

US

Birch Bay

Bellingham

Salt Spring I.

Swartz Bay

VICTORIA

Anacortes

Mt. Vernon

Thetis I.

Kuper I.

Galiano I.

STRAIT OF GEORGIA

Chemainus

Vesuvius

Long Harbour

Sturdies Bay

Village Bay

Mayne I.

Crofton

Salt Spring I.

Fulford Harbour

Otter Bay

Saturna I.

Pender I.

CANADA US

Mill Bay

Swartz Bay

Sidney

Strait of Juan de Fuca

Juan de Fuca

Port Townsend

Everett

Clinton

Vancouver Island

Brentwood Bay

Victoria

WASHINGTON

Port Angeles

15 km

| B.C. Ferry Routes |
| U.S. Ferry Routes |

30 km

SEATTLE

peninsula, is Robert's Bank, a coal loading area. Here you see trains, piles of coal, cranes, derricks, and containers, and usually a freighter tied up to receive the goods. At night the strings of lights add an ethe-real air of beauty that is not so obvious during the day.

To the southeast of the ter-minal the suburbs of Tsawwassen stretch along the shore that curves out to Point Roberts, a small isolated peninsula that is part of the U.S. Here's the place where some Canadians nip over the border to gas up before head-ing for the ferry.

Most Swartz Bay traffic is now carried on the two super-ferries, the *Spirit of British Co-lumbia* and the *Spirit of Van-couver Island,* which are the newest and most comfortable ships in the BC fleet. On a full run, each carries around 470 vehicles and 2100 passengers.

The ferry heads out across the Strait of Georgia, crossing

an angle of U.S. waters, with fine northerly views to the Coast Mountains behind Vancouver, and southerly views to the San Juan Islands and—on a clear day—the spectacular snow-covered cone of Mount Baker in Washington State. Ahead is the long barrier of the outer Gulf Islands.

Watch for changes in the colour of the water when sailing across the Strait. The muddy water is from the Fraser River and the clearer water from the Pacific. There is a definite line before the colours mix. This is the most exposed part of the journey, and on windy days you may feel a little swell. Only occasionally is there a storm severe enough to bring traffic across the Strait to a halt for a few hours.

Once aboard, many passengers head for the restaurant in order to eat their meal while crossing the Strait of Georgia. Then, free to roam the decks, they can enjoy the spectacular scenery and wildlife while sailing through Active Pass and the islands.

The entrance to Active Pass is a narrow gap between the islands of Galiano and Mayne. The narrow channel, which has a double dogleg as well as some reefs, can carry up to 750,000 cubic metres of water a minute, and, as the only passage between the outer Islands for a long distance, carries a lot of traffic. The beauty of the islands, the concentrations of wildlife, and the diversity of water traffic makes this stretch the best time to be on deck.

Despite the non-stop activity of hundreds of boats sailing daily through Active Pass, this

Tsawwassen Terminal is an impressive sight

is not how it gained its name. It was named by Captain Richards of the British vessel HMS *Plumper* after an American survey vessel, the *Active*, which was the first recorded ship to sail through the pass. The pass is very attractive to wildlife, particularly outside the summer, and depending on season you may see 100 or more bald eagles, up to 10,000 Bonaparte's gulls and 7,000 Brandt's cormorants, 2,500 Pacific loons and 1,000 western grebes. It is not uncommon to see porpoises or a pod of orcas, and Steller's sea lions

favour Helen Point. Salmon feed in the waters at both ends of the pass in the summer, so small boats gather in large numbers.

Emerging from Active Pass below Mount Galiano, there is a view to port into Village Bay, Mayne terminal for the ferry. From now on, the view is full of islands, as the ferry heads forward into open water. As you come clear of Galiano and Mayne, there are extensive views through the long narrow seaway that runs inside the outer islands. To the northwest, Trincomali Chan-

Vancouver

A view of Granville Island and the beautiful city of Vancouver

THE WEST COAST'S largest port city is situated adjacent to the delta of the Fraser River, and set against a backdrop of spectacular mountains. It is surrounded by other municipalities, and the region has a total population of approximately 1.5 million. Vancouver is a vibrant, booming city that has everything: discos, theatres and other nightlife, beaches and sea walks, Stanley Park (one of the most extensive inner city green spaces of any city in Canada), major malls and fabulous restaurants, skiing at the top of nearby Grouse Mountain, and striking art galleries, museums and multicultural neighbourhoods.

Visit the Museum of Anthropology to view an inspiring collection of Native art, including splendid totem poles, the Maritime Museum to sense the impact of the ocean, and the Aquarium to explore the wonders beneath the sea. A trip through Chinatown or one of the Asian malls gives a sense of Vancouver's connection to the rest of the Pacific Rim and beyond. But don't forget a dockside walk, for Vancouver is not just a tourist city but the working and beating heart of provincial industry. You'll see working ships from around the world entering the Burrard Inlet under Lion's Gate Bridge, competing for space with the luxury cruise ships heading out into the Inside Passage to Alaska. The seabus will take you across Burrard Inlet; on False Creek, harbour ferries putter to and fro between English Bay and Granville market, and the skytrain and bus service can take you quickly and easily to almost any point of this varied metropolis.

Superferries meet in Active Pass

nel is bounded by Galiano, Prevost and Salt Spring islands, whereas to the southeast, Navy Channel runs between Mayne and Pender. Trincomali is named after a British naval vessel, while Navy Channel was so named because the Navy used the cliffs there for target practice.

The ferry moves forward between Prevost and Pender, and gradually Captain Passage comes into view to starboard, leading into Ganges Harbour, with its many small islets and views of mountainous Salt Spring beyond. Opposite, Plumper Sound runs along Pender's southwest shore, with distant views of the San Juans. As the ferry nears Swartz Bay, it passes other islands, taking one of a number of possible routes. One is Portland Island with Princess Margaret Marine Park, opposite the deep inlet of Fulford Harbour on Salt Spring. A cluster

of smaller islands close to the dock are relatively heavily populated, though the smallest are just big enough to be someone's "dream island"— with room for one house perched on top and a boathouse by the shore.

At Swartz Bay Terminal you have reached the northern tip of the Saanich Peninsula, part of Vancouver Island. This terminal is almost as busy as Tsawwassen, as it serves six destinations by several different routes. You can change here for Galiano, Mayne, Pender, Salt Spring, and Saturna islands (though some of them might be more easily reached from Tsawwassen). Substantial rebuilding has made this perhaps the best-equipped terminal from a passenger's point of view, and it has most of the same facilities as Tsawwassen. Leaving the terminal, you can connect with Washington State Ferries in

Sidney, head on to Victoria, or set off up Vancouver Island to many possible destinations.

Ferry Facts

FREQUENCY OF SERVICE varies from day to day and season to season. Peak periods and holidays normally have extra services: always consult current timetables or phone for specific information.

- **Tsawwassen–Swartz Bay:** 1 hour 35 minutes, at least 8 trips per day each way.
- **Tsawwassen–Nanaimo:** 2 hours, about 8 trips per day each way.
- **Horseshoe Bay–Nanaimo:** 1 hour 35 minutes, 8 trips per day each way.
- **Comox–Powell River:** 1 hour 15 minutes, about 4 trips per day each way.
- **Brentwood Bay–Mill Bay:** 25 minutes, 9 trips per day each way.

On the Bridge with Captain Myerscough

"**WHEN I FIRST** come up to the bridge in the early morning, all is quiet, with just a few flickering lights on the computers to remind me that the ship is a huge creature talking to itself." Captain Myerscough is Master of the *Spirit of Vancouver Island* this morning, quietly in charge but also making sure we appreciate the poetry of his work as well as the mechanics.

He shows us the mechanisms that allow the bridge to be the nerve centre of the whole vessel. Closed-circuit TV screens show the passenger and car decks at a glance. The Chief Officer walks round the ship and checks all the safety equipment while the second officer checks the battery of bridge equipment for navigation, safety, engines and auxiliaries. The Captain has a chat with the Chief Engineer down in the bowels of the ship. The cooks are busy preparing breakfast for the hungry passengers waiting on shore. "It's like a city coming alive."

A report comes of the total number of crew on board—determining the number of passengers that can be legally carried—and this information is conveyed to the tower at the terminal. The Chief Officer supervises loading, and then passes the shore's clearance to leave to the master. The watertight doors are closed, lines let go, the draft of the ship checked, and the superferry is on its way.

Captain Myerscough brings the superferry into dock

Weather information arrives continuously, marine traffic information is a phone call away, and the radar screens show everything close by. The chief officer cons the ship, giving

Window on the water through the floor of the bridge

direction to the quartermaster, while the Captain reminisces about his childhood near the great port of Liverpool in England, his apprenticeship with the Cunard Line, his experience with the navy, and his nearly thirty years with BC Ferries. When the first superferry was delivered, of course, no one had first-hand experience with them; Captain Myerscough was one of three captains who worked together on the maiden voyage. The first time he was in charge of one was in the dark, and taking an unfamiliar run into Esquimalt.

As we approach Swartz Bay the Captain takes over at the separate docking equipment installed on the wing of the bridge, where a window at his feet shows the water and dock. He brings the huge vessel smoothly to rest at the dock, with as much elegance as if he was parking a mini in an empty street. Some 2000 passengers are safely delivered, and the responsibility is off his shoulders for a few hours. So how does he relax? "I sail a 22-foot Westerly. And I have trouble in reverse."

HIGHLIGHTS OF ACTIVE PASS from east to west. In this direction, Mayne Island is to port, and Galiano to starboard.

1. Georgina Point Lighthouse (Mayne) keeps a watchful eye on the east entrance to Active Pass. The resident keeper has witnessed some near misses in Active Pass and has been instrumental in rescuing several boaters in difficulty. A 1784 English penny found on the point suggests that crew members of Captain Vancouver's ex-pedition landed here.

2. Sturdies Bay (Galiano) is the terminal for ferries to the island. You may see one docked there as you pass. Under certain conditions, it can be exposed to heavy seas, so occasionally ferries must use the older, more sheltered dock at Montague Harbour.

3. Miner's Bay, the only sheltered bay in the pass with a small village of the same name nestled along the shore. Here, weary would-be gold miners rested during the long row from Vancouver Island to the mainland to join the 1860 Fraser Valley goldrush.

4. The tall cliffs beyond Mary Anne Point (Galiano) are topped by beautiful Bluffs Park which has walking trails along the cliffs giving spectacular high views of the pass and the islands beyond.

5. The wooded area on the southern shore (Mayne) is an Indian Reserve. It is a favourite place for bald eagles resting beside one of their favorite fishing grounds. Scan the tallest trees and look for a white patch. This indicates an eagle is perched there; the white patch is its "bald" head. It is not unusual to see about 20 eagles scattered around the shores of Active Pass; the highest count is over 100.

6. Georgeson Bay (Galiano) is named for an early island family. Archaeological sites here have been dated back to 3,000 years ago.

7. Collinson Point (Galiano) marks the western end of the pass. Here, in August 1970, three people were killed when the ferry Queen of Victoria collided with Russian freighter Sergey Yesenin in thick fog. Dramatic photographs show the bows of the freighter piercing the ferry almost to midline.

8. Helen Point (Mayne) is a favourite salmon-fishing spot, and dozens of small boats can gather here, but sometimes have to scurry out of the way of the ferries.

This aerial photograph shows Active Pass looking southeast from Galiano Island

Looking south over the Swartz Bay Terminal with a superferry in dock.

Victoria

Victoria from the harbour

VICTORIA IS SITUATED 18 miles down Patricia Bay highway from the Swartz Bay Ferry Terminal. This "city of gardens" and provincial capital is one of the prettiest cities in Canada. Victoria is small in scale; you can walk across the city centre within half an hour, and, on a pleasantly human scale, it has only a few high-rises. Many of the office buildings have kept their historic facades and the "old town" area is full of boutiques, restaurants, and renovated arcades and alleys.

Imposingly situated at the head of the Inner Harbour is the elegant Empress Hotel, the place for Olde English afternoon tea. There is lots of parking in this central area and just about everything worth seeing is within easy walking reach. Check out the magnificent Royal British Columbia Museum with its incredible walk-through habitat displays and wonderful collection of Native artifacts. Beacon Hill Park has rose gardens and cliff walks with wonderful views

across the strait to the mountains of the Olympic Peninsula. There is a variety of restaurants, and the oldest Chinatown in Canada is accessed through a spectacular Chinese gate. Galleries, gardens, and a veritable plethora of shops can be visited by foot, rickshaw, or horse and carriage. English-style double-decker buses offer scenic tours around the marine drive and to some more distant attractions such as the famous Butchart Gardens.

Brentwood Bay to Mill Bay

A useful short cut for traffic heading "up island" from Swartz Bay is this little ferry across Saanich Inlet. You will need to follow signs or use a map to find it, about 15 minutes away from leaving the terminal, but you can save an hour or more in the drive around the south end of the inlet. If you would be likely to hit Victoria at rush hour or there is snow on the Malahat Pass out of the capital, you could save more time. However, it is only a small ferry, and if you can't get on you might lose time instead of gaining it.

Tsawwassen to Nanaimo

The Mid-Island Express is a relatively new service, started in 1990, which attracted 1.4 million passengers and 600,000 vehicles in its first full year. It is particularly helpful for people travelling from the Lower Mainland to Nanaimo and points north, allowing them to bypass the traffic of Vancouver. The journey up the length of Strait of Georgia is pleasant, with distant views of both the mainland mountains and the outer shores of Galiano, Valdes and Gabriola Islands, with the higher parts of Vancouver Island visible beyond. As it does not approach the shores closely except near the terminals, however, it is without the dramatic views of most of the other routes.

Horseshoe Bay to Nanaimo

Horseshoe Bay terminal be-

Approaching Horseshoe Bay

gan with the Black Ball Line, which pioneered service up the Sunshine Coast. In a sheltered bay near the end of a peninsula in West Vancouver, it opens onto Howe Sound and is sheltered by Bowen Island from the open strait. Ferries from Horseshoe Bay cross the sound to Langdale, serve Bowen, and cross the strait to Nanaimo. This is the second most popular crossing of the strait, carrying over 3 million passengers and over 1 million vehicles in 1993–94.

The terminal is small in relation to its load, and situated at the base of a steep hill, with little room to ex-

Nanaimo

The Bastion is a reminder of Nanaimo's past

THIS SPRAWLING CENTRAL Vancouver Island city is booming. Known as "mall city" for the almost continuous mall developments along the Island Highway, Nanaimo is a shopper's paradise, with competing malls offering bargains galore. The Departure Bay Ferry Terminal is near the centre of the city, and Nanaimo is the jumping-off point for all destinations north and west on Vancouver Island. Nanaimo is an interesting city with a fascinating social and industrial history.

Following a report by a native visiting Victoria, Hudson's Bay men first opened up coalfields in Nanaimo in 1853, employing First Nations. Nanaimo's famous Bastion was built in the same year to protect miners from possible native attack. When ships were powered by coal, and local vessels were powered by coal brought from South Wales down the Atlantic and round the Horn, a local source of supply was likely to be useful. In 1854 a group of 23 miners and their families were recruited from Brierly Hill Colliery in Staffordshire, England, and were brought out on a six-month voyage on the *Princess Royal*. For well into this century Nanaimo was a coal town, producing 1 million tonnes in 1923. As the coal became harder to work, however, lumbering has taken over as the major industry.

pand. Fortunately the main route is served by large ferries (*Queen of Cowichan*, for instance, will take 1466 passengers and 362 vehicles). Snack bar and cafeteria provide a good choice of food, though not as extensive as the superferries. There is a giftshop and other facilities. There are good views from the window seats: the starboard side is better for views in the first half, and the port side for the second half of the journey. On deck there are areas of seating sheltered by windbreaks.

Leaving the bay, there are glimpses up Howe Sound, which once provided access to industrial developments such as the Britannia Beach mine, which produced 48 million tons of ore (mainly copper and zinc) between 1905 and 1947. Highway 99 up the east side of Howe Sound is subject to winter rockfalls, and can be blocked for long periods, so a ferry dock has been developed in Porteau Cove Provincial Park for an emergency ferry ser-

Ferry Funny

A GRANDMOTHER travelling as a foot passenger, in charge of some extremely lively grandchildren, got them safely aboard and playing happily. As the ship sailed, she sat back with a sigh of relief only to jolt upright with the dreadful realization she had left the baby sleeping peacefully at the terminal.

The Captain rose to the occasion, sailed back into port, and the sleeping infant was safely retrieved.

Queen of Cowichan *and the Coast Mountains*

vice when it proves necessary. The main ferry route passes Bowen Island, initially developed at the turn of the century as a vacation resort for Vancouverites.

For the main part of the voyage, the ferry runs below the spectacular Coast Mountains. In the distance, outer Gulf islands Gabriola and Valdes gradually come clearer as Nanaimo is neared.

As the ferry pulls out into the strait, the islands of Texada and Lasqueti come into view to the north; they were once seen as possible stepping stones for railway bridges on Canada's transcontinental railroad.

Approaching Gabriola Island, the lighthouse of Entrance Island can be seen close to the north shore. Look south as Gabriola is passed, and the Gabriola ferry may be visible. The ferry continues round the north point of Newcastle Island, and then Nanaimo comes into view, climbing the hillsides of Vancouver Island.

The dock at Departure Bay, Nanaimo has a bit more space than Horseshoe Bay. Although close to the city centre, there are few facilities in the immediate vicinity. Head south into the town for the Gabriola ferry, which leaves from a different dock.

Powell River to Comox

The shortest crossing of the strait, initiated in 1965, connects the forestry town of Powell River with the agricultural area of Comox. The ferry has views of mountains on both sides, as well as north to Quadra and Cortes islands, and (after running past the northern end of Texada Island) south to Denman and Hornby islands and beyond. If you are lucky, a wait at Comox can be enlivened by aerobatic displays from the nearby military base.

Superferry funnel

7. Island Hopping

Queen of Cumberland *serves the southern Gulf Islands*

Many islands cluster along the eastern shore of Vancouver Island; the largest and most populated are served by BC Ferries, while a few others can be reached by private passenger services. Each island has its own character and charm; the most accessible are rapidly growing residential areas, and all attract visitors in search of quiet rural atmosphere, history and wildlife, and land- and water-based recreation. Most are referred to as "gulf islands"; the name has stuck from earlier times when what is now known as the Strait of Georgia was thought to be closed at the northern end.

The southern Gulf Islands form a complex archipelago east of the lowest part of the island. The most southerly of these (Galiano, Mayne, Saturna, Pender, and Salt Spring) can be reached from both Tsawwassen and Swartz Bay, while ferries from Vancouver Island serve the west coast of Salt Spring, Thetis and Kuper, and Gabriola.

Further "up island," other ferries serve some of the more scattered northern Gulf Islands, Denman and Hornby, Quadra and Cortes. A private passenger ferry will get you to Lasqueti. Even farther up, a triangular route serves Malcolm Island (Sointula) and Cormorant Island (Alert Bay) in Queen Charlotte Strait. The islands are all in the rain shadow of the mountains on Vancouver Island; the southern ones are drier and warmer, and you will find cooler temperatures and more rain as you move north and west. However, all can have beautiful weather and are worth a visit at any time.

From the mainland, the southern islands are reached from Tsawwassen, starting along the same route as the Tsawwassen to Swartz Bay ferries (Chapter 5), but stopping at Galiano, Mayne, and Pender and terminating at Long Harbour on Salt Spring. Saturna is reached by a change at Mayne or Pender. This ferry route is the only ferry that you have to book before travelling if you need space for a vehicle—otherwise the chances are that you won't get on. Most travellers visiting the islands bring their cars and as there are only two ferries a day (morning and evening) from Tsawwassen to the islands, space is limited. In the summer the weekend sailings are sometimes booked up several weeks in advance, so mid-week travel is advisable whenever possible. On long weekends even foot passengers have been left behind. From Swartz Bay, near Sidney, smaller ferries serve the same islands. The shortest route leads into Fulford Harbour on Salt Spring. Other ferries cruise along the south shore of Salt Spring, calling at one or more of Pender, Mayne, Saturna and Galiano.

The Strait of Georgia from Dionisio Point, Galiano

Southern Gulf Islands

Galiano is the first stop from Tsawwassen, so is a favourite of Vancouverites looking for a break from city life. One of several islands named for the Spanish explorers of these waters, Galiano has many attractive parks and offers a variety of educational programs about the islands. There are plenty of places to stay and eat, but only a few galleries and studios.

Mayne is one of several islands named for the British naval officers who surveyed the area over a century ago. The major settlement, Miner's Bay, got its name in the Fraser River gold rush, and still houses the oldest pub in B.C., Springwater Lodge. It has accommodation and restaurants, and numerous nice beaches, but almost no parks.

A leisurely cruise down Navy Channel between Mayne and Pender and into Plumper Sound leads to Saturna, a secluded island with few facilities. Though one of the quietest islands, Saturna throws the biggest party in the southern islands; once a year the marine park at Winter Cove is the scene of a gigantic lamb barbecue that draws visitors from all over the coast.

Pender is a single island, that has been divided in two

Ferry Facts

FREQUENCY OF SERVICE varies from day to day and season to season: always consult current timetables or phone for specific information (including all inter-island services).

- **Tsawwassen–Galiano:** 50 minutes, normally 2 trips per day.
- **Tsawwassen–Mayne:** 1 hour 25 minutes, normally 2 trips per day.
- **Tsawwassen–Saturna:** 2 hours 20 minutes up, with a transfer, 1 or 2 trips per day.
- **Tsawwassen–Pender:** 2 hours, normally 2 trips per day.
- **Tsawwassen–Salt Spring (Long Harbour):** 2 hours up, normally 2 trips per day.
- **Swartz Bay–Salt Spring (Fulford):** 35 minutes, 10 trips per day
- **Swartz Bay–Pender:** 35 minutes, 4 trips per day.
- **Swartz Bay–Saturna:** 1 hour 15 minutes, 3 or more trips per day.
- **Swartz Bay–Mayne:** 1 hour 35 minutes, about 4 trips per day.
- **Swartz Bay–Galiano:** 1 hour 10 minutes up, around 4 trips per day.
- **Vancouver Island (Crofton)–Salt Spring (Vesuvius):** 20 minutes, about 14 trips per day.
- **Vancouver Island (Chemainus)–Thetis & Kuper:** 30 minutes up, about 10 trips per day.
- **Vancouver Island (Nanaimo)–Gabriola:** 20 minutes, around 17 trips per day.
- **Vancouver Island (Buckley Bay)–Denman:** 10 minutes, 18 trips per day.
- **Denman–Hornby:** 10 minutes, 15 trips per day.
- **Vancouver Island (Campbell River)–Quadra:** 10 minutes, 17 trips per day.
- **Quadra–Cortes:** 45 minutes, about 5 trips per day.
- **Vancouver Island (Port McNeill)–Alert Bay & Sointula:** 30 to 45 minutes, 10 trips per day.

Village Bay, Mayne Island

by a small canal dredged across the portage to enable steam ships to shorten their journey through the Gulf Islands. North and South Pender were reunited by a bridge built in 1955. A mix of older settlements, beaches, parks, and studios along the narrow country roads is attractive to many visitors. There is plenty of accommodation, but less choice of places to eat.

Salt Spring is the biggest of the southern Gulf Islands, and has the largest population, most services and facilities (including more than 30 studios, and many places to stay and eat). It is served by three separate ferry routes. Yet it is far from suburban: it has the highest mountain and largest lake in the islands, and there are plenty of trails. The town of Ganges is the only substantial community in the southern islands and (depending on where you approach it from) is either a charming rural experience or a bit too urban for comfort—after all, it has one way streets.

Vancouver Island to Southern Gulf Islands

North of Swartz Bay, other island ferries depart from the east coast of Vancouver Island. Some ferry terminals are so close they can be seen from the main highway; others require a detour into secondary roads, but all are well signed. The first, from Crofton, goes to Vesuvius on the west coast of Salt Spring. The large pulp mill at Crofton is a (sometimes smelly) reminder of the importance of B.C.'s forest industry.

The ferry to Thetis and Ku-

Loading at night, Otter Bay, Pender Island

per islands leaves from the small tourist town of Chemainus, which rescued itself from decline as a logging town by creating a series of mural paintings which have made it a prime tourist attraction.

During a pleasant crossing of Stuart Channel, you can look south to the Crofton pulp mill and Salt Spring, and over Thetis to Bodega Ridge on Galiano. The ferry threads small rocky islets and touches

Gulf Island cruise

IF YOU WISH to sample the Gulf Islands, several of the smaller ones can be seen from a delightful three- or four-hour cruise by ferry from Swartz Bay, Vancouver Island.

Check the timetable for "Day Trip from Swartz Bay." This mini Gulf Islands cruise generally starts mid-morning from Swartz Bay and returns three or more hours later. This is a wonderful opportunity to choose a fine day, pack a picnic (the smaller ferries have snack bar food only) and travel as a foot passenger. For a few dollars you can enjoy the scenery as the ferry noses in-

to the small docks on the beautiful archipelago of islands strung out beyond the Saanich Peninsula. For a full day trip, hop off at either Mayne or Pender and catch one of the later ferries back, but check to make sure that there is another one on the day you are travelling.

Islanders know this circular journey as "the milk run," and may use the same circular trip as a favourite break taken from individual islands. One group of island women takes it monthly and refers to it as the "PMS cruise"—Pender, Mayne, and Saturna of course.

The Nanaimo Bastion is displayed on the Queen of Nanaimo

at both islands, alternating its first stop. From Kuper dock you can look into Telegraph Harbour with its marinas.

Thetis and Kuper were two parts of a single island that was separated by a canal dredged in 1905. The two islands have had very different histories, for Kuper continued the ancient tradition of native settlement and remains an Indian Reserve, whereas Thetis was developed as a pioneer settlement by newcomers.

Thetis Island enjoys one of the smallest populations and the least development of any Gulf Island with a regular ferry service, but is a pleasant day trip for the visitor. The island has a number of interesting and attractive features, but has no parks or walking trails. Accommodation is limited and there are no campsites. Most of the island facilities are within easy walking distance

of the Thetis ferry dock, so it is possible to enjoy the island as a foot passenger.

From the ferry dock on Nanaimo Harbour (opposite the downtown Harbour Park Mall), the high sandstone cliffs of Gabriola can be clearly seen. The ferry to Gabriola is perhaps the only one to be immortalized in the name of a novel—Malcolm Lowry's *October Ferry to Gabriola*. Leaving harbour, it provides views of Newcastle Island Marine Park, and skirts Protection Island (which has its own passenger ferry, the *Protection Connection*). The regular ferries make Gabriola an easy day trip destination from Nanaimo, although the island also offers a variety of accommodations for those who wish

Ferry Funny

AN OLD CAR broke down just short of the correct ferry line-up. Helpful passengers pushed it into place and opened up the hood. After a short discussion, some of the passengers ran to their various cars, hauled out tools and converged again upon the ailing vehicle. Within minutes pieces of the engine's innards were strewed on the ground around the car. Then came the announcement that the ferry was docking. Work went into overdrive and bits of engine were replaced at high speed. As the line of waiting cars moved forward, the driver scooped up the last few extraneous nuts and bolts no one had found a home for, slung them into the back seat, fired up and drove onto the ferry to a round of applause.

Rolf Leben stacks the deck

A TALL SWEDE with a German name, Rolf is known in the fleet as "one of the best guys to 'stack the deck," and can apparently safely and efficiently load more cars than anyone else. Rolf never gets enough of the sea, and he and his wife actually live on an old wooden 80-foot boat, *The Granby,* that he moves up and down the coast according to where his work base is and what ship he's on.

For some time he was working out of the Queen Charlottes on the *Kwuna,* the most northerly BC Ferry. His own boat was moored 15 feet away from the *Kwuna's* berth at Skidegate, so when in dock Rolf could go home for lunch. *The Granby* is easily recognized as it has a flat parking space on the cabin roof so Rolf can drive his car off the

Rolf Leben on the bridge, Queen of the North

dock and take it with him on the boat. After working the northern ferries, boat and car were headed to Salt Spring for winter work at Fulford Harbour.

Queen of Nanaimo *approaches Salt Spring Island*

to stay for a while. Gabriola is an island of beautiful beaches, sculptured shorelines, and attractive parks. The famous Malaspina Galleries were noted as a natural wonder by Spanish sailors (perhaps before any other tourist attraction in British Columbia), and the island has many petroglyphs, carved by natives in ancient times. It has plenty of services and some interesting artists' studios.

Northern Gulf Islands

Denman and Hornby are accessed from Buckley Bay (12 miles or 20 km south of Courtenay which is approximately half-way up Vancouver Island). If you've time, you can find Fanny Bay Oysters tucked away under the gas station, and stock up with wonderful seafood. The first ferry ride leads to Denman, which has a rural agricultural flavor; its topography lent it-

self to farming, and many of the old farms and orchards remain. There is only one main store, and a couple of parks. There is one small campsite (10 spots only) and a few bed

& breakfasts. Drive across Denman to Gravelly Bay to catch the ferry to Hornby.

Hornby Island has a sculpted coast, which offers more interest to the visitor,

Profile of a commuter

"**FIFTEEN LONG** years. It's a long time to commute on the ferries. But not the longest, there's another man who's been doing it for 25."

"I know the crews and I know the captains. On my run there are three regular captains. We always know who's on, there's Captain Delay, Captain On-Time, and Captain By-The-Book. Actually no matter who's on, the evening ferry is always late."

"No. Once the ferry was early. There must have been a following wind and we arrived at Sturdies Bay 20 minutes ahead of time. There was no one around and no one got off. The ferry hung around and still no

passengers came, so we actually departed a few minutes earlier and headed into Active Pass. We got half-way through the Pass when there was a commotion. A passenger had slept through his Sturdies Bay stop. We turned around and went back to Sturdies so he could disembark. Wouldn't you know it, we arrived at Pender 45 minutes late."

"Commuters are like a club. We meet on the ferries every week and chat and swap horror stories about jobs. We get to know the crew members and see photos of their kids and families. When crew members retire, or get transferred, or have babies, we all sign a card for them."

Ganges on Salt Spring from the air, Galiano in the distance

with several areas of unusual rock formations and some beautiful bays. Hornby Island is best known as an artistic community; there are several art and craft studios scattered across the island and several well-known potters, and it is known for its music festivals. The wonderfully imaginative community hall is also worth visiting. Hornby has a variety of accommodations, but limited eating opportunities.

Opposite Campbell River is another pair of islands, Quadra and Cortes. These are the two most accessible of the complex of islands and peninsulas that almost blocks the northwestern end of the Strait of Georgia. The narrows be-

Gabriola ferry arrives at Nanaimo

tween the islands funnel all the boat traffic travelling north from Vancouver and Puget Sound, and so can be exciting for ship watchers.

A short ferry trip from downtown Campbell River

serves Quadra. As you cross you can see the southern tip of the island, the primary residential area for both Natives and other residents. At one time this island was the northern limit of Salish terri-

Fighting with property

THE COMPLEX WEST coast native custom of the potlatch involved giving away huge quantities of goods on occasions marked with ceremonies, dances, and displays of art. It served many functions, including enhancing status, cementing relations between groups, and marking important occasions, but also could be used to humiliate rival elders in a process that has been called "fighting with property."

The custom baffled Victorian missionaries and civil servants, who managed to get it banned in 1885. Potlatching continued in secret, and eventually arrests were made in 1913 and 1919. Some natives were fined, others got suspended sentences on condition they wouldn't potlatch any more. In 1921 the Kwakiutl held several potlatches. At one that lasted 6 days, Chief Dan Cranmer invited several hundred guests,

Potlatch at Alert Bay

and the gifts included 24 canoes, 400 Hudson's Bay blankets, and 1,000 sacks of flour. Twenty-two natives were arrested and sent to prison, and the gifts and ceremonial paraphernalia were impounded. Over 450 ceremonial items, including 20 coppers and dozens of masks, were shipped to museums in Ottawa and Toronto, and some were sold in

New York. Awareness of the discriminative nature of the legislation grew, but it was not until 1951 that the law was repealed. In 1979 and 1980 the National Museum repatriated much of this important material, and it was used to form the collections of the Cape Mudge Museum on Quadra and U'Mista Cultural Centre at Alert Bay.

The ferry arrives at Thetis

tory, but its native inhabitants now belong to the group now known as Kwakwaka'wakw. Older forms of the name used by non-natives include Kwak-iutl and Kwagiulth, the latter preserved in the name of the Kwagiulth Museum in the heart of the main native settlement of Cape Mudge Village, which is laid out in traditional fashion along the waterfront. Nearby Tsa-Kwa-Luten Lodge is a native-owned hotel that serves traditional meals and sometimes

Ferry Funny

IN THE DAYS BEFORE BC Ferries, passengers and automotives were not the only things transported. One ship also loaded a small herd of cows that were then barricaded in below deck. During the voyage the cows broke down the barrier, charged up the stairwell and proceeded to stampede around the decks with the crew in hot pursuit. The passengers sat back and watched the fun.

presents native dancing. Outside the reserve, many interesting and unusual houses can be glimpsed through the trees. Most of the island services (including several stores) are found in the vicinity of the ferry terminal at Quathiaski Cove, and there is another settlement and services across the island at Heriot Bay, the ferry terminal for Cortes Island. Several lodges and bed & breakfasts provide accommodation, and there is a choice of restaurants. There is only one small park, but Quadra has a real feeling of wilderness in the northern part of the island, with some spectacular trails among the lakes and up the China Mountains, and there are rumours of major new park development here.

The ferry from Heriot Bay sails past the end of Rebecca Spit Marine Park and crosses the northern end of the Strait of Georgia to Cortes Island, another 45 minutes away. Here, some accommodation

and services are available, but the island is basically a quiet retreat. It is perhaps best known for Hollyhock Farm, which offers workshops "in the practical, creative and healing arts." There is also a beautiful marine park, and the many sheltered bays are popular with canoeists and sailors exploring the Desolation Sound area.

Queen Charlotte Strait Islands

Until the northern part of the Island Highway was completed, Kelsey Bay was the southern terminus of the Inside Passage ferry route. Port McNeill is the basis for a triangular route serving Alert Bay on Cormorant Island and Sointula on Malcolm Island. Although close together the communities are incredibly different in atmosphere and history.

Alert Bay is a bustling fishing and tourist town, with a variety of services, famous for its U'mista Cultural Centre, a

Gulls—Grey Wings Over the Sea

MORE THAN A DOZEN species of gull occur on the B.C. coast, but the odds are you will usually be looking at a glaucous-winged gull. (The term "sea"gull, by the way, is a misnomer, as many species of gulls spend their time inland, and may breed and winter there.) With a population of some 25,000 breeding pairs, Glaucous-winged gulls are by far the commonest on the coast, and may be seen following fishing vessels, or clustering round schools of fish. Traditionally their favourite breeding places are on small islands: the biggest colony in recent years seems to be the one on Mandarte Island, near Sidney, with over 2,300 pairs. You will recognize an adult by a combination of characters: several gulls have a yellow bill with a red spot, and pink legs and feet, but the glaucous-winged is the only one that also has gray wing tips. Young birds are darker, with pinkish-brown mottling all over the body.

Populations have increased greatly as they have learned to coexist with people. They started nesting on buildings about 1960, and downtown Vancouver now has around 500 nesting pairs. Around the ferry dock these gulls are scavengers, eagerly gulping down any offering passengers leave around. But be careful of your sandwiches—they will help themselves if you're not watching. Even if *you* don't like gulls there *are* those that do: the glaucous-winged gull is now the principal prey species for the bald eagle.

proud showcase for the culture of the Kwakwaka'wakw Nation. Nowhere else along the coast is the presence of the aboriginal people so vibrantly felt as in Alert Bay, and the combination of its island setting, cultural centre and totem poles make it a destination well worth visiting.

Sointula is a small Finnish settlement whose name means "harmony." It started out in 1901 as a utopian community that would follow the teachings of writer Matti Kurrika, who had already gone to Australia. Local Finns raised money to bring Kurrika to B.C. to help found the new colony. Unfortunately the settlement was unable to live up to its name, and, after several scandals and arguments over money, eventually fell apart

four years later over the issue of free love. From this rocky beginning has developed a peaceful and picturesque fishing village with the Finnish presence still visible in store names and baked goods, and occasionally heard in shops and cafés. There is a museum and limited accommodation, but it's not really a tourist town.

Explosion at Ripple Rock

SEYMOUR NARROWS, just up from Campbell River, was notorious among seamen for tidal streams up to 15 knots. In 1875 the US warship *Wachusett* was destroyed in a whirlpool, and over the next 80 years, 24 large vessels and more than 100 smaller ones were lost here. The main

problem was Ripple Rock, which rose 400 feet from the sea bottom in mid channel, but did not reach the surface.

In 1943 attempts to moor a barge over it and drill into the rock were unsuccessful. Eventually, a shaft was dug on nearby Maude Island, then a tunnel un-

der the rapids, and a honeycomb of passages inside the rock. The holes were packed with 2.75 million pounds of dynamite, and the charge was fired on April 7, 1958. The explosion was, at the time, the largest man-made non-nuclear blast in history, and Ripple Rock was no longer a problem.

8. Sunshine Coast

Sunset at Lund, the end of the Sunshine Coast road

The Sunshine Coast boasts one of the highest annual number of hours of sunshine in all of Canada—up to 2,400 hours of sunshine, compared to Vancouver's 1,900. In the early 1920s, the Union Steam Company used the slogan "Sunshine and Sea-Charm along Holiday Shores on the Gulf Coast," and the short version, Sunshine Coast, has been with us ever since. Obviously many people agree: BC Ferries carry more than four million passengers and nearly two million vehicles on the Sunshine Coast routes every year, making it the second biggest traffic area in the system. More recently, the stretch of coast from Gibsons, at the mouth of Howe Sound, to Powell River has attracted many people, who have built cottages, summer homes, or retirement homes.

The scenery is spectacular: there are fjords to cross by ferry, islands, snow-capped mountains, and much boating traffic. Highway 101 up the coast takes you through seaside villages, along stretches of beach, and up mountain sides, with high peaks on one side and a steep dropoff to the ocean on the other. Many campgrounds, parks, and resorts entice the visitor to stay and play. Maverick Coach Lines provides a bus service between Vancouver and Powell River. Drivers should note that the trip from Horseshoe Bay to Powell River takes about 4.5–5 hours.

Bowen Island

Part of the Coast Range of mountains, Bowen Island is hilly and was once thickly forested. Its first settlers were loggers. Later, level areas were farmed, and for a while there was a brickyard and even an explosives factory. By the First World War, the island was becoming a resort for Vancouver residents, and the Union Steamship Company devel-

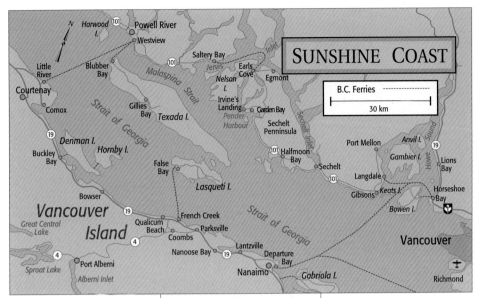

SUNSHINE COAST

B.C. Ferries
30 km

oped a recreational complex in the area around Snug Bay, the present ferry terminal. In recent decades it has grown fast, and Bowen politics are often split between those who want development of urban services and those who wish to keep it as rural as possible.

Vancouver to Sechelt

Begin your journey up the Sunshine Coast at the Horseshoe Bay ferry terminal. Travel time to Horseshoe Bay from Vancouver is about one hour, but this can be much longer during the weekday rush hour. The ferry, usually the spacious *Queen of Cowichan*, takes you between Bowen and Gambier islands to the ferry dock at Langdale. The view north up

Bowen Island was developed as a resort by Union Steamships

Ferry travellers crossing Howe Sound

Howe Sound, seen from the ferry, is truly awesome. The road journey along Highway 101 begins at Langdale and quickly takes you to the seaside village of Gibsons, where everyone seems to have a home with an ocean view. Watch for Molly's Reach Restaurant, familiar to the many people around the world who have seen Gibsons and its environs through episodes of the television program, *The Beachcombers*.

Sechelt to Powell River

Sechelt is the main service centre for the Sunshine Coast and sits on a flat piece of land between the end of Sechelt Inlet and the Strait of Georgia. Travelling north, you encounter places with enchanting names like Half Moon Bay, Smuggler Cove, and Buccaneer Bay. You may be tempted to divert from the main road to explore aptly named routes such as the Red Roof Road. Highway 101 then takes you around the edge of Pender Harbour—the major boating and recreation centre between Vancouver and Desolation Sound. Over two dozen marinas dot the shore of this major salmon fishing area.

You eventually arrive at Earls Cove, where a ferry will take you across the mouth of Jervis Inlet, another fjord that is much longer and narrower than Howe Sound. Highway 101 picks up again at Saltery Bay, and takes you to Powell River after an hour of travel. The region is more rugged than the lower Sunshine Coast, and distinctly less developed. Arriving at Powell River, a busy pulp mill town, the visitor has several choices. One is to continue on to the end of the Sunshine Coast road to Lund and the beginning of Desolation Sound. A second is a ferry to rugged Texada Island. Lastly, you can take the ferry from Powell River across to Comox on Vancouver Island, where road routes link you up with numerous other ferry routes.

Ferry Facts

FREQUENCY OF SERVICE varies: always consult current timetables or phone for specific information.

- **Horseshoe Bay–Bowen Island:** 20 minutes, about 15 trips per day.
- **Horseshoe Bay–Langdale:** 40 minutes, about 8 trips per day.
- **Earls Cove–Saltery Bay:** 50 minutes, about 8 trips per day.
- **Powell River–Texada:** 35 minutes, about 10 trips per day.

9. Cruising the Inside Passage

Heading north through the Inside Passage

If you enjoy a long voyage through an endlessly changing wild landscape, the trip known as "The Inside Passage" is an ideal 15-hour cruise and, deservedly, the ferry route favoured by international visitors. The ship is comfortable, the food the best on the ferry system, and the scenery is incredibly spectacular. It attracts 70,000 passengers a year, mainly during the warmer months.

In summer, passengers settle to read, chat with fellow travellers from around the world, or prowl the outer decks with cameras and video-recorders, anxious not to miss a moment of the ever changing landscape. On a fine day, the scenery is the prime attraction. The open waters of the sound are succeeded by narrow channels, and fjords branch off in all directions. Island after island, with their cliffs, bays, mountains and waterfalls, provide a continuous parade of wild beauty. Wildlife varies with the seasons, but something is always present. Eagles perch in large trees, seals bask on rocks, porpoises and dolphins sport in the ship's wake, and pods of killer whales may be seen. Sometimes even larger whales swim by, taking a side trip on their migrations.

Human presence is mostly apparent in the passing boats: streams of fishing boats come from or head to a herring or salmon opening; a tug pulls a log boom or barge at barely perceptible speed; pleasure craft thread the channels, and sometimes an Alaska Cruise liner will share the narrows, its passengers lining the rails to watch the ferry sharing the same scenery for a fraction of the price.

Occasionally, there is a lighthouse or buoy to mark the passage, but otherwise

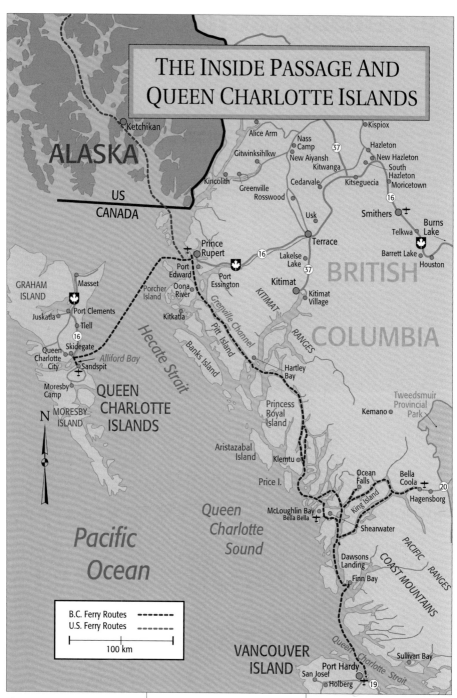

THE INSIDE PASSAGE AND QUEEN CHARLOTTE ISLANDS

ALASKA

US
CANADA

Ketchikan

Kispiox
Alice Arm
Nass Camp
New Aiyansh
Gitwinksihlkw
Kitwanga
Hazleton
New Hazleton
South Hazleton
Moricetown
Kincolith
Cedarvale
Kitseguecia
Greenville
Rosswood
Smithers
Burns Lake
Telkwa
Usk
Barrett Lake
Houston

GRAHAM ISLAND
Masset
Port Edward
Porcher Island
Oona River
Port Essington
Prince Rupert
Terrace
Lakelse Lake
BRITISH

Juskatla
Port Clements
Tlell
Kitkatla
Kitimat
Kitimat Village

Queen Charlotte City
Skidegate
Alliford Bay
Sandspit
Hecate Strait
Banks Island
Pitt Island
Grenville Channel
Hartley Bay
KITIMAT RANGES
COLUMBIA

Moresby Camp
QUEEN CHARLOTTE ISLANDS
MORESBY ISLAND

N

Princess Royal Island
Kemano
Tweedsmuir Provincial Park

Aristazabal Island
Klemtu
Price I.
Ocean Falls
Bella Coola
Hagensborg

Pacific Ocean

Queen Charlotte Sound
McLoughlin Bay
Bella Bella
King Island
Shearwater
PACIFIC RANGES
COAST MOUNTAINS

Dawsons Landing
Finn Bay

B.C. Ferry Routes
U.S. Ferry Routes
100 km

VANCOUVER ISLAND
San Josef
Port Hardy
Holberg
Queen Charlotte Strait
Sullivan Bay

only an occasional old cannery, a few tiny fishing villages or logging camps show any human presence on this dramatic landscape. The tiny town of Bella Bella is the largest community in this area where a recently built ferry dock at McLoughlin Bay al-

Fishing boats cluster at Port Hardy

lows vehicles to be loaded and unloaded.

In fine weather the landscape is splendid, but many times parts of it may be obscured by fog, creating its own misty magic and real-life Hollywood effects of drifting cloud. The very nature of this northern coast means the weather varies—but even the rain is awe-inspiring.

Booking Your Trip

The Inside Passage is a route where advance booking is important. It is a long way to go to either Prince Rupert or Port Hardy and find out there is no room on the ferry. Several key summer sailings fill to capacity. On the other hand, we spoke to passengers who had booked only 24 hours before

sailing. Although short notice is possible, it is far better to assure your passage by making a reservation in advance.

To make a booking, phone, write or fax to head office with your name, address, telephone, number of your party (include ages of children), the day you prefer to depart (with alternatives if possible), your requirements for cabin or day-room accommodation, and details of your vehicle (over 6' 8" high, over 20' long). Cabins

Discovery Coast Passage

A NEW NORTHERN SERVICE is available, connecting Port Hardy with a number of hitherto remote northern communities on the mainland. Stopovers are possible, but you should book ahead for the limited accommodation. Associated packages may also be booked with BC Ferries.

Service is provided by a revamped *Queen of Chilliwack*—it has enhanced food service and a licensed lounge. At Finn Bay you can connect with local transportation to Rivers Inlet. Namu offers the oldest archeological site on the B.C. coast and a

historic fish packing plant. At McLoughlin Bay you can connect with special boat tours, fishing trips, or the Shearwater Resort. Ocean Falls offers a historic walking tour of a former mill town, at Klemtu you can see native dancing, and in Bella Coola a local museum illustrates the Norwegian background of the historic community.

Note that not all ports are serviced on each voyage. To find out where each ferry will stop, get the specific leaflet or phone BC Ferries for more detailed information.

Ferry Facts

FREQUENCY OF service varies; always consult current timetables or phone for specific information.

- **Port Hardy–Prince Rupert:** May–September: 15 hours, one trip northbound and southbound on alternate days.
- **Tsawwassen–Port Hardy–Prince Rupert:** 2 positioning cruises per year: northbound late May; southbound end of September.

Cruising the Inside Passage

are small, with room for two or four berths and some luggage. The cheapest ones are below the car decks. They are not essential unless you are taking a round trip on the same ferry, but if you want a safe place to stow your belongings, and a place to snooze undisturbed, they are strongly recommended.

Join the *Queen of the North* either at Port Hardy or Prince Rupert by public transport, an organized bus tour, or private car. At both terminals you should book accommodation in advance; if you are travelling as foot passengers through Prince Rupert, ask if the hotel will meet the ferry, as it may be some distance away.

Be sure you know which ship you are booked on. The best passenger facilities are on the *Queen of the North*. The *Queen of Prince Rupert* is an older, more rugged ship that usually services the Queen Charlottes. She has her own character but does not have the elegance and comfort of the *Queen of the North*.

Port Hardy

Port Hardy is a small logging, mining, and fishing town, and it is worth arriving early enough to explore. There are shore walks, a small museum, an interesting wharf, and a variety of eating places.

The town is highly geared to assist the Inside Passage ferry passengers. The Travel Infocentre will book accom-modation for you, and coordinate bus transportation if you register on arrival. All the bed & breakfast establishments, as well as the hotels, function around the hours the ferries arrive and depart. Breakfast is cheerfully served at 5:30 am ready for the 7:30 am ferry departure, by a host or hostess who may have welcomed guests at 1 a.m. from the arriving ferry. If you have registered for pick-up, the bus arrives at your door, and will deliver you to the ferry terminal at Bear Cove, across the bay from Port Hardy.

The town is equally organized for the return trip which doesn't arrive until 12:30 am. The minibus meets the ferry, and delivers sleepy passengers

ONE OF THE HIGHEST-ranking female officers in BC Ferries, First Officer Janice Lloyd had nearly completed her Master's Certificate when we talked to her. Janice started out in the fleet's catering department and rapidly worked her way up to the position of Chief Steward, but she'd always wanted to be on deck. "That wasn't a realistic goal when I first started."

After Chief Steward, her next prospect was to join management and go on shore, but Janice didn't want this, so after *much* discussion, she got herself moved sideways and downward, corporately speaking, and became an Ordinary Seaman. "I worked my way up again as a seaman to my present position. There was no policy against female officers but it wasn't easy and I ran the gamut of nicknames and jokes."

Janice Lloyd cons the ship

Now she is settled in on the top rungs, and, when we visited the bridge was very efficiently "conning" the ship through a narrow pass. ("Con" means Control Of Navigation; Janice was calling out the course to steer to the quarter-master.)

Janice has incredible energy and a thirst for knowledge. "I never feel I know enough. I'm not in a hurry to become a Master. I have to take the time to get experience."

First Nations at Bella Bella, around 1913

to their various places of rest. Because of this organization, the Port Hardy folk know when the ferry is late and plan accordingly. Rest assured, if they know you are coming, you will be welcomed, even in the early hours of the morning.

Queen of the North

The Inside Passage is the longest BC Ferry trip, so you will have time to get to know your vessel. The *Queen of the North* is an elegant vessel originally built for the Swedish Stena line. There are comfortable lounges with reclining chairs—easy for snoozing as well as sightseeing. (Be aware that choice ferry seats in the lounge cannot be "saved" while you are out on deck—we've seen yelling matches when there is a full complement of passengers). If you're backpacking, ask where the storage racks for packs are located. There is a licensed lounge with live entertainment in the evening, and beer and wine are also available in the dining room. A bookstore, video game room, and children's playroom offer alternatives to the constantly changing scenery. Movies are shown in the lounge a couple of times during the trip. If you haven't booked a cabin in advance, there may still be some

Ferry Funny

ON THE LONGER northern routes, ferry personnel who live on board follow their own recreational pursuits. One Captain, while he was a junior officer, used to play the bagpipes in the emergency generator room. In order to play a trick on him, the engineers found a way to start the generator by remote control. Next time he started to play, the machine suddenly came to life. In due course he received a formal memo from the Chief Engineer, asking him to refrain from practicing there, as the sound of the bagpipes ws causing the generator to start.

Lighthouse at Boat Bluff

Mackenzie at Bella Coola

At the head of Dean Channel is the modern community of Bella Coola. Nearby is a landmark in the history of North America: the place where fur trader Alexander Mackenzie (1764-1820), with a small party of voyageurs, was the first to cross the mainland of North America. It was in July, 1793, 12 years before Lewis and Clark reached the Pacific across what is now the United States, that Mackenzie reached the western point of his historic journey. After a hazardous trip over the Rocky Mountains from the Peace River area (the farthest west, then considered part of Canada), Mackenzie wrote an inscription on a boulder where the Bella Coola River empties into the ocean. In his journal, he recorded the event.

"From Canada, by land"

"I now mixed up some vermilion in melted grease, and inscribed, in large characters, on the South-East face of the rock on which we had slept last night, this brief memorial. 'Alexander Mackenzie, from Canada, by land, the twenty-second of July, one thousand seven hundred and ninety-three.'" The presumed site of the lost inscription is now in Sir Alexander Mackenzie Provincial Park, where the inscription has been reinscribed.

available— but don't count on it.

The most fun is on deck, watching the endless parade of scenery. Under normal circumstances, you don't need to worry about seasickness: the Inside Passage is very sheltered, and the only time you are likely to feel the swell is when the ferry briefly crosses Queen Charlotte Sound. Just make sure you wear several layers of clothing that can be added or removed as needed. Depending on the weather and your position on the ship, you may be removing enough clothing to sun bathe, or wishing you'd brought another sweater as the sea breezes chill you to the bone.

Port Hardy to Bella Bella

Heading out of Port Hardy in the early morning, the ferry crosses the largest stretch of open sea on the whole trip,

the mouth of Queen Charlotte Strait. The swell from the west might have come all the way from Kamchatka, and sometimes it feels like it— winter storms have a reputation here.

After about an hour and a half, you are in the Inside Passage, a series of channels between offshore islands and the mainland coast that provides shelter for vessels from the power of the Pacific. Channels lead off on either side—passages leading on one side to the Pacific; on the other, deep fjords thrusting into the mainland mountains. Most settlements on this coast are at the head of a fjord, too deep inland to be seen from the Inside Passage.

Bella Bella

Five hours sailing from Port Hardy is the isolated community of Bella Bella, and you

may be lucky enough to travel on a ferry that stops there.

The name Bella Bella comes from an English language corruption of the name of the local native group, the Bil Billa, also known as the Heiltsuk people. This is a thriving community of approximately 680 residents, whose main industries are logging and fishing. The large community centre, with art work on the side, is seen prominently in the middle of town, as are the band-operated store and hotel. You can also easily identify the new hospital and the church. Until recently, Bella Bella had only a single wharf, so the ferry had to dock sideways, and could not load or unload any vehicles bigger than a bicycle.

Views of the Inside Passage

Bella Bella to Prince Rupert

A short distance north of Bella Bella, the ferry crosses Milbanke Sound, a short stretch open to the ocean. Ivory Island, opposite the sound, has a lighthouse built on a bare rock. One lightkeeper's wife managed to convince the Light Services Supply Depot to ship in dirt so that she could create a garden.

Soon the ferry is in sheltered waters again. The channel is divided by Sarah Island, and the ferry passes close to Boat Bluff lighthouse. Some 10 hours from Port Hardy, wide Douglas Channel heads inland, leading to the aluminum-smelting town of Kitimat. The ferry sails along narrow Grenville Channel for about two hours—perhaps the most spectacular part of the route.

Prince Rupert

Prince Rupert, B.C.'s most northernly major port, is actually situated on Kaien Island in the Inside Passage, a fact not obvious to the average visitor, who usually explores only the central area of the city. A dozen or so hotels and a couple of campgrounds suit most traveller's needs, but may all be full at peak periods.

Prince Rupert's history belongs entirely to the 20th century, for it was planned in 1906, as the dream of Charles M. Hays, general manager of the Grand Trunk Pacific Railway, for a coast terminus to compete with Vancouver and the CPR and CNR. The town was laid out in a heavily wooded area while the railroad was advancing to the coast. Unfortunately, in 1912 Hays went down in the *Titanic,* with all the plans for the port in his head. It was another two years before the first train made it to the coast.

Thriving businesses included fishing for salmon and halibut (for a while Prince Rupert was known as the world's halibut capital), as well as lumbering and some shipbuilding, but the town's fortunes fluctuated with the railway.

Although it is a working town, there are some very interesting sights for tourists. The waterside area, particularly picturesque Cow Bay, is worth a walk. In the past it was the site of a floating logging camp and the place cattle were driven off the boat and made to swim ashore. Now an

67

Cow Bay has a popular marina

attractive wharf-side strip, which has been redone for tourists, features a floating bed & breakfast and a couple of appealing eating places. There are antique shops in the area and interesting views of the yacht club and the islands across the bay.

The Museum of Northern British Columbia is worth a visit, to see some exceptionally good examples of West Coast native artifacts from various parts of northern B.C., including work by various members of the highly regarded Edenshaw family. There's a fine collection of argillite, some rare coppers, carvings, and a cast of a petroglyph telling the story of a human figure who fell from the sky. It also contains the Travel Infocentre, and runs harbour tours of archaeological sites.

Helitours, fishing charters, and whale-watching tours are also readily available. The city has quite a collection of totem poles from the Queen Charlottes and the hinterland, though they are scattered through the parks, and have sometimes been heavily restored. Just minutes from the downtown area is a gondola lift that carries visitors 1,850 ft above the city. Arrival at the ski chalet gives access to a boardwalk and fabulous views. On a clear day it's reported you can see across to the Queen Charlottes, but certainly the islands around Prince Rupert and Southern Alaska are reward enough.

North Pacific Cannery Village Museum

The old mess hall is now a coffee shop

THE NORTH PACIFIC Cannery Village Museum, a 30-minute drive away from Prince Rupert, is at Port Edward, on the banks of the Skeena River. Built in 1889, it was managed by a succession of companies until 1981, when it was closed down. It was declared a National Heritage Site in 1989. It is the oldest surviving cannery of the many that once supported the salmon fishing industry in a scatter of sites along the coast. It is being restored by a group of local people who recognized the importance of saving some of their industrial heritage, and who now operate as the North Pacific Cannery Museum Society.

Once served by sailing boats and powered by steam, the plant went to diesel ships and electrical power. It was manned—mainly in summer—by a great diversity of staff, including Scandinavian fishermen, British managers, Japanese boat-builders, Chinese labourers, and First Nations people who did the cleaning and canning. Each group had its own

Cannery wharf and machine shop

housing. Now it is possible to see some buildings dating from each period of the site, along with the wharf, netloft, bunkhouses, offices, and houses.

10. Queen Charlotte Islands

Haida Gwaii beaches are embellished with driftwood

Captain George Dixon was the first European navigator to sail round these beautiful remote islands. They have been named after his ship, which in turn honoured Queen Charlotte, the wife of George II of England. Although Queen Charlotte Islands is still the official name, the Islands are now often referred to as Haida Gwaii, their usual native name, as an acknowledgement of the Haida's 9,000 years of occupancy. They are also commonly nicknamed the Misty Islands for the prevailing weather, which is warm and moist, with spectacular low-cloud effects interspersed with bright sunny periods. They combine magnificent wilderness and semi-wilderness with remains of an ancient heritage, vigorous rebirth of Haida culture, good roads and reasonable tourist amenities in the settled northeast region, and incredibly friendly, outgoing people.

Visit Haida Gwaii for wild beaches and dense forests, for Haida canoes and totem poles, for excellent fishing and cruising, for good seafood and good company. Don't expect five-star accommodation; most is clean and adequate, but not fancy. Dress for changeable weather: rugged clothing that accepts rain or sun, and boots that don't mind mud, rock, or sand. Then you are set for one of the best vacations you can have. On the northern Graham Island, there are beautiful campsites and accommodation from Queen Charlotte City to Masset. The southern Moresby Island is only accessible by public road in the northeast. The rest, and more remote islands can be visited only by plane or boat. The Haida people ask only one thing: remember this is their sacred homeland, so tread softly, be a visitor who leaves no trace, and you will be welcomed back. As on many small islands, things here change quickly, and people and businesses come and go. Local information may change overnight, so a local contact can be the key to the success of your trip.

The islands are accessed by ferry from Prince Rupert, so they can easily be added to an Inside Passage trip. However, the trip involves crossing the largest stretch of open sea in the ferry system, and can be rough. A short ferry hop linking the two largest islands is the farthest-flung route in the BC system.

Prince Rupert to Skidegate

The *Queen of Prince Rupert* is the usual summer ferry from the mainland. She is older than the *Queen of the North* and not so glamorous. But she's sturdy, steady, and ready to load everything from passengers to cattle and furniture vans, to dangerous goods. She's the reliable working boat that's the all-important link between Haida Gwaii and the outside world. Almost everything of importance comes to these islands via *'The Rupert."* The cavernous car deck eagerly swallows up the large trucks, and the crew swarms around, bracing them with steel posts, not just blocking wheels as on the southern routes, to make sure the cargo won't shift.

Packs and lug-

Fly agaric is a common fungus

gage can be checked in by foot passengers, airport style, at Rupert, and reclaimed from the van on arrival at the Skidegate terminal. It is important to make sure you have everything you need for the voyage with you, as checked baggage is not accessible in transit. Vehicles on the car deck are accessible for periods announced by the crew. The *Rupert* has more than adequate passenger facilities: there's both a dining room and a cafeteria, and the food is great. There's a licensed lounge as well as a

regular lounge and movies for the passengers who are tired of a long stretch of ocean. The biggest attraction on this ship is the passengers. The islands are small and everyone you meet on board you will meet again, probably several times, during your visit to Haida Gwaii. Stories shared on board will facilitate your visit and expand your knowledge of this remote corner of the world.

After a stretch of protected water, the ferry heads out to cross Hecate Strait, the most open stretch of water on the BC Ferries' routes. On stormy days the trip can take a lot longer than the scheduled eight hours. On a clear day there are distant views of the Alaskan islands to the north. The ferry travels along the eastern shore of Graham Island, and arrives at a small terminal

Balancing Rock was left by glacial ice

at the southern end, just outside the village of Skidegate.

Visiting Haida Gwaii

Although you are not entirely in the wilderness, visiting Haida Gwaii takes a bit more planning than the average vacation. Accommodation on the islands is limited, so book ahead. Main centres are Queen Charlotte City (unincorporated), the commercial and administrative centre of the islands, New Masset at the other end of the island, some of the smaller communities in between, and Sandspit and a few other spots on Moresby Island. Skidegate and Old Masset are native settlements.

Not far from the ferry is a helpful tourist information centre run out of a private home on the main road to Queen Charlotte City. It's a somewhat amazing set-up as it's not just a travel information centre but also "Joy's Island Jewellers." Park on the driveway and walk in. Joy will be delighted to see you, will give you a full travel spiel, and phone and make on-the-spot accommodation bookings for you if necessary. There are published guide-

The end of a storm at Port Clements

books, but some of the most useful information on the islands is available in a locally produced *Guide to the Queen Charlotte Islands,* which is updated annually and contains maps of all the accessible communities, as well as detailed in-

Skidegate to Alliford Bay

The Kwuna docks at Skidegate

FREQUENCY OF SERVICE varies from season to season: always consult current timetables or phone for specific information.

- **Prince Rupert–Skidegate:** 8 hours. June to September: sailings most days in each direction. October to May: Three sailings weekly from each port.
- **Skidegate–Alliford Bay:** 20 minutes, 12 trips per day.

ON ARRIVAL AT Skidegate, travellers for Moresby Island find themselves right beside the northern terminal for the Alliford Bay ferry, the tiny *Kwuna,* which takes cars and foot passengers hourly across to Moresby Island. Surprisingly, this short route carries more passengers each year than any of the other northern routes. The 20-minute trip offers good bird watching, and spec-

tacular views of the mist-enshrouded islands and channels, and is worth a round trip, even if you have no plans for the southern island. From the Alliford Bay terminus, a short road leads to Sandspit, where the airport and a few services form a base for travel by air to the mainland and by helicopter to some of the southern Haida village sites.

formation on places of interest. It's available by mail; ask for the price of the current edition when you phone for information.

Beyond the paved roads is an extensive system of gravel logging roads, which are accessible with permission from the logging companies. Car and truck rentals are available in some centres.

Much of Moresby Island and adjacent areas is a national park reserve, Gwaii Haanas. All visitors must register with Canadian Parks services, who jointly administer the area with the Council of the Haida Nation, assisted by the Haida Watchmen. In these remote places are the abandoned villages, with rows of leaning totem poles that make the Charlottes magical. The area is not accessible by road or without permission. Local adventure tours by helicopter and float plane, and fishing and kayak tours, are available. Some can be contacted when you arrive, but, to avoid disappointment, it's best to book ahead.

Graham Island

The name of Queen Charlotte City is deceiving, as it is a community with one street. However there is a variety of accommodation, several good places to eat, a grocery store and bank, and several interesting galleries.

The Queen Charlotte Islands Museum is located just outside Skidegate. It's a very impressive small museum with some totems and other outstanding artifacts, as well as a gallery of changing exhibitions focused on local artists, photographers, and film makers. The museum has a whale-watching viewpoint, for Haida Gwaii is one of the best places to watch gray whales on their spring migration, and many visitors come to the Charlottes especially to see them. They travel from their wintering grounds in Baja California, Mexico up to

Emily Carr on the Queen Charlottes

"A PICNIC WITH the Indians and old Billie dog" was Emily's description of this photo, taken at Cha'atl in the Queen Charlottes in 1912.

Emily Carr, B.C.'s famous pioneer woman artist, loved to paint wilderness and totem poles. The Queen Charlotte Islands were a favourite place, which she visited first in 1912, soon after returning from her training in Europe. The following year she exhibited almost 200 paintings in Vancouver, and lectured on the paintings and her experiences. Some admired the impressionist-influenced paintings, but no one bought them, and she had to give up her studio and move back to Victoria, "all the art smashed out of me flat."

She was not able to return to the Charlottes until 1928, and has left a vivid account of adventures in a letter to Eric Brown of the National Gallery. "Last Wednesday I contracted with an

Emily Carr picnics at Cha'atl

Indian who had a gas boat to take me to three villages way off over bad waters." Carr was seasick, and was marooned at Skedans with a native girl when the engine failed and the boat drifted off in a storm. "We scratched up some kind of a meal and prepared to spend the night on the beach in the pouring rain. It was a wild spot—quite a few totems, dense undergrowth. I would have enjoyed it." A party of Norwegians rescued artist and boat, and she continued. "I was sick. I lay flat on my back on the top of the fish hatch and did not care what happened." By now she was much surer of her skills, and on return painted some of her finest work.

A modern totem at the Queen Charlotte Islands Museum

Alaska. They swim east of these islands on their northward journey. During their southward fall migration, they pass these islands on the westward side. If a pod is seen on the ferry crossing, the Captain will announce it.

Nearby Skidegate was once a spectacular Haida village with rows of poles now seen only in old photographs and Emily Carr paintings. Skidegate is still essentially a Haida village, but a modern one. Many of the old poles were chopped down at the insistence of missionaries, or removed to museums. One fine new pole carved by Bill Reid stands on the shore in front of the band administration offices. These offices are built in the style of a traditional longhouse, and inside there are some old photographs and paintings. Ask the receptionist for a tour. Farther down the road there is a replica of an important and beautiful entrance carving over the cemetery gate.

Visitors are welcome to look at the entrance but are asked not to enter the cemetery itself without permission from the band offices.

The main highway heads north past Tlell, and the inland Port Clements to Masset. The white folk refer to Masset as their settlement and the nearby Haida village as Old Masset. The Haida refer to their village as Massett (the real spelling— the post office dropped one "t" so it wouldn't be confused with Merritt in the B.C. interior) and the white settlement as New Massett. Some maps refer to the white settlement as Masset and the native village as Haida!

A nature reserve behind New Masset attracts water birds, while Old Masset has a number of modern poles. A road runs east into Naikoon Provincial Park, where Tow Hill is a striking lookout on spectacular beaches.

Reg Davidson: Haida Artist

REG DAVIDSON IS A member of a long and important family line of Haidas; his ancestors include the Edenshaw and Davidson families. Many of the Edenshaws and Davidsons were carvers, and at the age of 14 Reg apprenticed with his brother, the famous artist and carver Robert Davidson, thus learning the craft in the traditional manner. Reg gradually expanded his skill and knowledge and eventually began to take the traditional shapes and forms and reassemble them in his own way, thus evolving an art style that is unmistakably his, while still Haida.

Reg has to live in two worlds,

Reg Davidson at home

not always complementary. In Massett he is Reggie, though his house is "sort of fancy" with the signs of the frog and eagle clans carved on the fence and a cappuccino machine perking away in the kitchen. In Vancouver he is artist Reg Davidson, featured at art galleries and openings, demonstrating carvings at the museums and travelling internationally. (His next project is to head over to China to carve a pole as a gift from Canada.) He encourages his daughter to complete her university in Vancouver, but gives up his Vancouver home to return to Massett. For Reg and his art are centered here, in a quiet village on misty Haida Gwaii, the sacred land of his people.

Reference

Recommended Reading

Many books on B.C. are partly or wholly about the coast. We present here a limited number that are particularly useful. To save space, we have listed only one author for each; places of publication are in B.C. unless otherwise indicated. A selection of field guides to marine and forest life are useful companions for any ferry trip.

Passengers enjoy the sunshine

ARTS

Davidson, Robert. 1994. *Eagle Transforming. The Art of Robert Davidson.* Douglas & McIntyre. 164p.

Shadbolt, Doris. 1979. *The Art of Emily Carr.* Clarke, Irwin/Douglas & McIntyre. 223p.

FERRIES

Bannerman, Gary and Patricia. 1985. *The Ships of British Columbia. An Illustrated History of the British Columbia Ferry Corporation.* Hancock House. 176p.

Griffiths, Garth. 1967. *Dogwood Fleet: the story of the B.C. Ferry Authority from 1958.* Cadieux & Griffiths Ltd. 118p.

FIRST NATIONS

Kramer, Pat. 1994. *Native Sites in Western Canada.* Altitude Publishing. 160p.

Kramer, Pat. 1995. *Totem Poles.* Altitude Publishing. 112p.

Woodcock, George. 1977. *Peoples of the Coast. The Indians of the Pacific Northwest.* Edmonton: Hurtig. 223p.

HISTORY

Graham, Donald. 1986. *Lights of the Inside Passage. A History of British Columbia's Lighthouses and their Keepers.* Harbour Publishing. 266p.

Lillard, Charles. 1986. *Seven Shillings a Year. The History of Vancouver Island.* Horsdal & Shubart. 246p.

Rushton, Gerald A. 1974. *Whistle Up the Inlet. The Union Steamship Story.* J.J. Douglas. 236p.

White, Howard (Ed.) Ongoing. *Raincoast Chronicles.* Harbour Publishing. (A fascinating series of magazines about coast life, available in cumulative volumes).

Woodcock, George. 1990. *British Columbia, A History of the Province.* Douglas & McIntyre. 288p.

INSIDE PASSAGE

BC Ferries. 1993. *Your Guide to BC Ferries Inside Passage.* 22p.

Upton, Joe. 1992. *Journeys Through the Inside Passage. Seafaring Adventures Along the Coast of British Columbia and Alaska.* Whitecap Books. 189p.

NATURE

Campbell, Elaine C. et al. n.d. *Waterbirds of the Strait of Georgia.* British Columbia Waterfowl Society. 60p.

Ford, John K.B. et al. 1994. *Killer Whales. The Natural History and Genealogy of Orcinus orca in British Columbia and Washington State.* University of British Columbia Press. 102p.

Yates, Steve. 1992. *Orcas, Eagles & Kings. A Popular Natural History of Georgia Strait & Puget Sound.* Seattle: Primavera Press. 236p.

NORTHERN GULF ISLANDS

Jones, Elaine. 1991. *The Northern Gulf Islands Explorer—The Outdoor Guide.* Whitecap Books. 194p.

PLACE NAMES

Walbran, John T. 1971. *British Columbia Coast Names.* Douglas & McIntyre. 546p.

QUEEN CHARLOTTES

Shave, Debbie et al. 1994. *Guide to the Queen Charlotte Islands.* Observer Publishing. 76p.

SOUTHERN GULF ISLANDS

Spalding, David A.E. et al. 1995. *The Southern Gulf Islands.* Altitude Publishing. 160p.

VANCOUVER

Vogel, Aynsley. 1993. *Vancouver.* Altitude Publishing. 352p.

VICTORIA

Grant, Peter. 1994. *Victoria from Sidney to Sooke.* Altitude Publishing. 164p.

Index

Photographic Credits

HISTORICAL IMAGES
B.C. Archives & Records Service
15 (G-04681), 18 (F-04179), 19 (F-04514), 52b (F-04182), 55 (D-05548), 57 (B-06902), 64 (H-07104), 65b (i-05476), 73 (F-07756)

CONTEMPORARY IMAGES
Airphoto 85 (Aerial Photographers International)
32
BC Ferries Corporation
59, 62
Chris Cheadle
front cover, back cover, 2, 30, 36-37, 38-39, 44, 46-47, 51
Douglas Leighton
33, 41
Georgina Montgomery and Associates
16, 28-29, 35a, 45, 48, 58, 80
Dennis Schmidt
8b, 11b, 14, 17, 26-27(a&b)
Esther Schmidt
13
Andrea Spalding
24, 49b, 53a, 63, 70, 71a
David Spalding
12, 21, 22, 34, 35b, 40, 42, 43a, 49a, 50, 52a, 56, 61, 65a, 66a, 67a and b, 68, 69a and b, 71b, 72b, 74a, 74b, 76
Ricardo Ordóñez
6, 8a, 10, 11a, 20, 23, 43b, 54, 75

About the Authors

Lawrence Pitt (left), Andrea Spalding, and David Spalding

Andrea and David Spalding and Lawrence Pitt all live on Pender Island, and have been users of the ferry system for many years. They have collaborated (with Georgina Montgomery) on another Altitude title, Southern Gulf Islands. Andrea and David are writers, performers, and consultants, and also run Arbutus Retreat Bed & Breakfast

Lawrence Pitt is an independent scientist and part-time university lecturer, and sails a small yacht—around crossing-ferry hours.

Acknowledgements

This book could not have been written without the enthusiastic support of many of the staff of BC Ferries, of the staff of the BC Provincial Archives, of friends who provided accommodation and information, and of residents and fellow travellers who have shared their knowledge, insights, and enthusiasms with us.

At BC Ferries, we would like to particularly acknowledge the efforts of Bill Bouchard, Arensha Garrison, George Jackson, and Pat Stephens to facilitate our work. At sea, we are deeply appreciative of Captains Bill McKechnie, Ted McMeekin, and David Myerscough, who invited us to their bridges, generously shared their expertise, and permitted us to bother their crew. A number of Chief Stewards paved our way, particularly Catherine Jefferies and Judy Mandin (who was stuck with us for the longest voyage). Many ferry personnel were interviewed and provided stories and insights that made the book possible; in addition to those who are specifically featured in the book, Steve Clapton, Philip McRae, Ray Jupe, and Stan Smith were particularly helpful. During our travels, Jean and Ramsay Attisha (Prince Rupert), Reg Davidson (Massett), and Jack and Sharleen Greenwood (Queen Charlotte City) were particularly generous with their assistance. Angela Southwood briefed us on the Queen Charlottes, and Patrick Verriour shared his insights.

At Altitude, the enthusiasm of publisher Stephen Hutchings and his staff have not only made the project possible, but consistently enjoyable.